SUCCESS IN PROGRAMMING

HOW TO GAIN RECOGNITION, POWER, AND INFLUENCE THROUGH PERSONAL BRANDING

Frédéric Harper

Apress®

Success in Programming: How to Gain Recognition, Power, and Influence through Personal Branding

Copyright © 2015 by Frédéric Harper

This work is subject to copyright. All rights are reserved by the Publisher, whether the whole or part of the material is concerned, specifically the rights of translation, reprinting, reuse of illustrations, recitation, broadcasting, reproduction on microfilms or in any other physical way, and transmission or information storage and retrieval, electronic adaptation, computer software, or by similar or dissimilar methodology now known or hereafter developed. Exempted from this legal reservation are brief excerpts in connection with reviews or scholarly analysis or material supplied specifically for the purpose of being entered and executed on a computer system, for exclusive use by the purchaser of the work. Duplication of this publication or parts thereof is permitted only under the provisions of the Copyright Law of the Publisher's location, in its current version, and permission for use must always be obtained from Springer. Permissions for use may be obtained through RightsLink at the Copyright Clearance Center. Violations are liable to prosecution under the respective Copyright Law.

ISBN-13 (pbk): 978-1-4842-0002-5

ISBN-13 (electronic): 978-1-4842-0001-8

Trademarked names, logos, and images may appear in this book. Rather than use a trademark symbol with every occurrence of a trademarked name, logo, or image we use the names, logos, and images only in an editorial fashion and to the benefit of the trademark owner, with no intention of infringement of the trademark.

The use in this publication of trade names, trademarks, service marks, and similar terms, even if they are not identified as such, is not to be taken as an expression of opinion as to whether or not they are subject to proprietary rights.

While the advice and information in this book are believed to be true and accurate at the date of publication, neither the authors nor the editors nor the publisher can accept any legal responsibility for any errors or omissions that may be made. The publisher makes no warranty, express or implied, with respect to the material contained herein.

Managing Director: Welmoed Spahr
Acquisitions Editor: Jeff Olson
Developmental Editor: Corbin Collins
Editorial Board: Steve Anglin, Mark Beckner, Gary Cornell, Louise Corrigan, James DeWolf, Jonathan Gennick, Robert Hutchinson, Michelle Lowman, James Markham, Matthew Moodie, Jeff Olson, Jeffrey Pepper, Douglas Pundick, Ben Renow-Clarke, Gwenan Spearing, Matt Wade, Steve Weiss
Coordinating Editor: Rita Fernando
Copy Editor: Laura Poole
Compositor: SPi Global
Indexer: SPi Global
Cover Designer: Anna Ishchenko

Distributed to the book trade worldwide by Springer Science+Business Media New York, 233 Spring Street, 6th Floor, New York, NY 10013. Phone 1-800-SPRINGER, fax (201) 348-4505, e-mail orders-ny@springer-sbm.com, or visit www.springeronline.com. Apress Media, LLC is a California LLC and the sole member (owner) is Springer Science + Business Media Finance Inc (SSBM Finance Inc). SSBM Finance Inc is a Delaware corporation.

For information on translations, please e-mail rights@apress.com, or visit www.apress.com.

Apress and friends of ED books may be purchased in bulk for academic, corporate, or promotional use. eBook versions and licenses are also available for most titles. For more information, reference our Special Bulk Sales–eBook Licensing web page at www.apress.com/bulk-sales.

Any source code or other supplementary materials referenced by the author in this text is available to readers at www.apress.com. For detailed information about how to locate your book's source code, go to www.apress.com/source-code/.

Apress Business: The Unbiased Source of Business Information

Apress business books provide essential information and practical advice, each written for practitioners by recognized experts. Busy managers and professionals in all areas of the business world—and at all levels of technical sophistication—look to our books for the actionable ideas and tools they need to solve problems, update and enhance their professional skills, make their work lives easier, and capitalize on opportunity.

Whatever the topic on the business spectrum—entrepreneurship, finance, sales, marketing, management, regulation, information technology, among others—Apress has been praised for providing the objective information and unbiased advice you need to excel in your daily work life. Our authors have no axes to grind; they understand they have one job only—to deliver up-to-date, accurate information simply, concisely, and with deep insight that addresses the real needs of our readers.

It is increasingly hard to find information—whether in the news media, on the Internet, and now all too often in books—that is even-handed and has your best interests at heart. We therefore hope that you enjoy this book, which has been carefully crafted to meet our standards of quality and unbiased coverage.

We are always interested in your feedback or ideas for new titles. Perhaps you'd even like to write a book yourself. Whatever the case, reach out to us at editorial@apress.com and an editor will respond swiftly. Incidentally, at the back of this book, you will find a list of useful related titles. Please visit us at www.apress.com to sign up for newsletters and discounts on future purchases.

The Apress Business Team

To the memory of Florian Villemure (1953–1999)

Contents

About the Author. ix
Acknowledgments xi
Introduction xiii

Chapter 1:   Personal What?. 1
Chapter 2:   I'm Not a Rock Star 9
Chapter 3:   Me, Myself, and I. 19
Chapter 4:   Defining Your Brand: Are You a Ninja, a Pirate,
                  or a Rock Star?. 33
Chapter 5:   Do Epic Stuff 51
Chapter 6:   Weapons of Choice 79
Chapter 7:   The Secret Ingredient: Your Tribe 115
Chapter 8:   Work Your Magic 137

Index 153

About the Author

Frédéric Harper started his career as a developer working with different technologies, focusing mostly on web and mobile development. In small enterprises, startups, as a freelancer, and in Fortune 500 companies, Fred possesses varied experience and is known for being a man of action. Extremely social, he spent years challenging the industry and showing the openness of companies you would not expect, like Microsoft. Now, as senior technical evangelist at Mozilla, Frédéric shares his passion about the open web and helps developers be successful with Firefox OS. With more than 100 talks under his belt, Fred shares his love and expertise in technologies around the world. Like a serial entrepreneur, he can't help himself: he likes to make his project ideas into reality. It's why he proudly produced a GeekFest in his city, started two podcasts, brought the FailCamp concept to Montreal, co-founded an HTML user group for a technical audience, created a networking group for developers, and more. In parallel with his other activities, Fred has been blogging for several years, now at outofcomfortzone.net, and proudly wears his Geek T-shirts that have become his trademark.

Acknowledgments

Thanks to my parents, Denise and Jacques, who are always there for me and who gave me my passion for computers: without you I would not be where I am today, *je vous aime*!

Thanks to the woman sharing my life, Émilie, who heard quite often in the last couple of months, "I can't, have to write." *Merci d'être présente dans ma vie!*

Thanks to my friends who always support me in my crazy projects, *je suis chanceux de vous avoir.*

A special thanks to Java, Belle, and Morgane, who "helped" me a lot in the writing of this book. After all, that's what cats are for.

Introduction

"What an amazing job you have," a developer recently told me during a break at a conference. "You seem so passionate about it. I wish I could be paid to do something I like, too." Sadly, he was not the first one to tell me something like this, and he won't be the last. How can great developers reach the next level and do what they like for a living? How come someone like me, an average developer, was able to get his dream job and be where he is today? Then it struck me: I know the secret sauce—it's personal branding!

Sharing is part of my DNA. I've always shared my knowledge, expertise, and passion with others. Why should I keep the formula that has been so lucrative for me a secret? I want to share what I know about personal branding with my fellow developers. I want to help people wake up on Mondays and be happy to go to work. I want to help others be as successful as I have been, no matter their definition of success. I began sharing the idea of thinking about yourself as a brand by giving talks at conferences. The feedback from the audience was astonishing, and I was only scratching the surface. They wanted more, they deserved more, and I wanted to give more. I wanted to educate as many developers as I could on personal branding.

To achieve my goal, I needed a way of reaching many developers—something a bit more structured than a series of blog posts. That's how the idea of writing a book came to mind. What you have in your hands now is the final result of putting that secret sauce into words. I decided to share with you part of my story, my failures, and my successes. From now on, when developers approach about achieving success in programming, I know I'll have the perfect recipe for them.

CHAPTER 1

Personal What?

What Is Personal Branding?

> [Personal branding is] the art of consistently presenting, online and offline, the essence of how you stand out from the crowd.
>
> —Paul Irish, Google Chrome advocate

Congratulations! By choosing this book, you have already made the first step in achieving some of your goals and reaching the next step in your career. Whether it's about getting a new job, reaching the next level in your company, earning a bigger pay check, or becoming a leader in your industry, personal branding is one of the keys that will help you achieve your goal.

This book is primarily written for developers—people who create software and write code every day for a living. No matter what your job is, if you're in a technical role, this book can help you. If you're a designer, architect, or systems administrator or do anything else involving technology, you'll have no problem following the examples here, even if some of them may not be directly applicable to the brand you want to build. In the end, personal branding isn't just for developers. It's for everyone.

You may think you need to be a seasoned old hand to think about your personal branding—that to reach the next level, you need to have many years of experience building software, creating wireframes, or designing websites. The truth is, experience does make it easier: you have a bigger network and a better idea of what you want to do next. But inexperience shouldn't stop you. This book is for everyone, whether you have 20 years of experience in the industry or started just 6 months ago. Are you still at school? No problem—that might even be a better time to start your brand because you're starting with a blank canvas, which makes some things less complicated.

Chapter 1 | Personal What?

From the first page of this book to the last, I want you to challenge me and evaluate everything I've written. I want you to not trust me! Why? Simply because *you* are the owner of your personal brand. The only person in the world—in the universe—who knows what's best for you, what can work, what won't, and where you want to go, is *you*.

As for me, my experience and my desire to share my passion about this topic bring me the opportunity to offer advice based on my successes and failures. Every word in this book has been written with your success in mind. I firmly believe that what I've written here is the best advice I can give to someone who wants to work on his or her brand. But every single one of us is unique. Life would be boring if we were all the same, right? So keep that in mind as you read this book, and feel free to take or leave what you please. This book is all about you, so make it yours and enjoy the journey.

In this first chapter, I demystify personal branding. What is it exactly? I explain the general concept of branding and deconstruct some of the misconceptions that may crop up when you try to think about yourself as a brand.

Let's Talk about Branding First

Can you recognize the brand shown in Figure 1-1, even though it's been altered to be made up of just circles? What brand comes to mind?

Figure 1-1. A well-known logo rendered with circles. (*Source:* Unevolved Brand #89. Logo by Graham Smith of ImJustCreative.com. Used with permission. https://flic.kr/p/8U5whB/)

Success in Programming

If you said Firefox, you win! (Sorry, I have no prize for you.) Why were you able to guess the logo in this modified form? Certainly not because I work at Mozilla, the company that owns the logo. You recognized it simply because it's a well-known piece of software. You may not even use the Firefox browser. You might not like it. But at least you recognize the logo. Now forget the logo. What words come to mind when you think about the Firefox browser? Let me do the exercise, too: *web standard, open source, free, sophisticated, security* . . .

Let's do it again. Do you know which company is represented by the deformed logo in Figure 1-2?

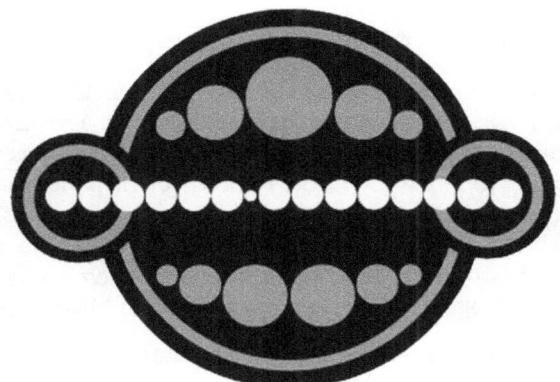

Figure 1-2. Another brand you may know, again made only with circles (*Source:* Unevolved Brand #91. Logo by Graham Smith of `ImJustCreative.com`. Used with permission. `https://flic.kr/p/8Vksmp`)

Did you think about Harley-Davidson? You got it. This logo is the visual signature of this iconic motorcycle company. Are you a fan of those vehicles? Maybe, maybe not, but even if you're not a biker, I'm pretty sure you recognize the logo. I'm not a motorcyclist, but I recognized it right away. Why was it so easy for me and probably you to do that? Simple: it's a well-known brand, even though it's not even a brand related to your type of job. You know Harley is the brand of choice for most serious bikers. The company also has great branding when it comes to quality. What words come to mind this time? Probably *quality, expensive, biker, rebel, loud* . . .

Let's try another one, this time with no visual cues. If I say the words *fast food*, what restaurants come to your mind first? McDonald's? KFC? Subway? Burger King? Your answer may vary depending on where you live, but in the end, the result is equivalent. If you do this exercise with people in your personal network, you'll probably end up with mostly the same answers.

Chapter 1 | Personal What?

If I say the words *healthy* and *sport*, which company first comes to mind? I bet you said Nike, because it's a company that makes sports gear, its swoosh logo is everywhere, and its mantra is "Just Do It." Nike's tagline pushes us to be more active and live a healthier life.

Even with no logos, we still got the same answer. That proves branding isn't about logos—it's about everything else. Here's what a marketing agency wants you to do: associate one word, sensation, feeling, image, or memory with their product, service, or store/restaurant. That is exactly what we'll try to achieve with personal branding.

Thinking about Yourself as a Brand

Personal branding is thinking about yourself as a brand. Of course, we won't be doing the same things as the companies we just talked about. We're not going to create ads for television or hire a marketing firm to help us with our image, and we're not going to make you into a rock singer or famous actor. In the end, the concept is the same. You want people to know you and associate you with something specific. You want to be one of the people who comes to mind when they think about that specific thing. You want them to be able to play the association game we played earlier, except instead of Nike, it'll be you.

Let's do another exercise, something more related to the day-to-day life of a developer. If I ask you to think about someone related to web standards in general, who comes to mind? There is a good chance you thought about Jeffrey Zeldman (most developers probably would). Here's why: his brand is so strong with regard to standards that he's known as the godfather of web standards.

Now identify the first person you think about related to CSS. Maybe Lea Verou? She's a developer with a high profile when it comes to cascading style sheet. She's worked at the W3C, has built many projects on GitHub, and has written a lot on her blog about CSS tricks, not to mention a book on the subject. She was part of the CSS working group and has done dozens of presentations on the topic.

It's not about being *the* uniquely dominant person for a specific topic. Many people can have a strong brand in any expertise. But you want to separate yourself from the herd in some way. Now try HTML5. I can think about many people who have a brand associated with this technology. I think about my friend Christian Heilmann from Mozilla, Paul Irish from Google, Bruce Lawson from Opera, and Remy Sharp, who runs his own company. If many names come to mind, does it mean their brands aren't good? Of course not! In some cases, when we go deeper into the topic, one name emerges from the crowd, but that doesn't mean that others don't have good brands, too.

Those examples were of international superstars in their domains, but personal branding is not just about superstardom. It depends on your goal: you may or may not want to reach that level, and this book isn't only about that. This will be your own journey, and you will determine which level you want to reach. Being a local star or the star of your company may be what you're looking for. It depends on what you want for yourself.

Let's play the game on a smaller scale. Think local, no matter what *local* means to you—it can be your company, your city, your network, or something else. What if I say the word *HTML5* again? If you aren't a web developer, choose any other technology—the word you pick doesn't matter, the exercise does. Personally, I think about my friend Mathieu Chartier, for many reasons. He's the president of a group called the W3Québec. Not affiliated with the W3C, this group promotes high standards and good practices on the web. He also started the HTML5mtl user group with me and another person from the community. I also think about my friend and co-worker Chris Mills from Mozilla. He wrote a book on CSS and has done many presentations on web technology. His daily job is to write documentation on HTML, CSS, and JavaScript on the Mozilla Developer Network.

What do these people have in common? They all did something amazing, and they all stand out from the crowd in some way. It was probably the same for you. Maybe your person wrote a book, gave a talk at a local conference, helped you solve a critical bug at work, started a user group, or contributed to an open-source project. In the end, they all did something good enough that you remember them—and you associate them with a specific technology or expertise. What do they have that others don't? Let's be bold and say that *their brand is strong.*

Your personal brand is about you, and only you:

- Who you are
- Who you want to be
- How you want to be seen
- **How people see you**
- What you do
- What you did
- What you didn't do
- What you'll do
- What you know
- What you don't know
- Your tribe

- Who you know
- Who knows you
- What you like
- What you don't like
- What you share

And more. It's about everything that defines you, from the languages you speak, to the way you do things, to your clothes, to the music you like! Anything can be part of your brand, and it will depend on your end goal, again. Let's be clear: it's not about selling yourself, it's about *marketing* yourself and your career. I put "How people see you" in bold in that list. That wasn't a layout issue. You'll see why I did that in upcoming chapters.

The following chapters will help you define your brand by thinking about and focusing on the who, what, and how. The *who* is about defining yourself and what you can bring to the table. The *what* is about defining your brand from the starting point—you: *what* your brand will be based on and *what* you want to achieve. Finally, I'll guide you on *how* achieve your goals and build your brand.

■ **Note** It's not *just* about you. Personal branding may be about you, but don't forget others. Many think personal branding is like jumping into a ring and fighting every opponent. That couldn't be more wrong. There is a full chapter about the importance of others. You don't need to step on others to achieve your goals, and others don't need to fail so you can succeed. You need to *always* play well with others. Never close the door, and always be there for others.

Personal Branding May Not Be for You

I should have told you this before: this book may not be for you. People who have a bread-and-butter job won't benefit from this book—you know, the job you do only to be able to pay your bills, have a roof over your head, and buy food. Of course, we're all working to survive in this world. At least we want to cover some part of our most basic needs. But there is a difference between a job you do because you have to make money and a job you do because you have to make money *and* it's what you like to do for a living. If you don't like what you're doing, there's no way you'll be able to build your personal brand and change your day-to-day work into an art form. You won't be able to go the extra mile. So why bother with personal branding? In this book, we'll see many elements that will help you have a successful personal brand, and one of them is loving what you do.

This book is not for you if you aren't ready to take your career to the next level. It's not for you if you don't want to fight the status quo. If you don't want to improve your situation, whether or not it's a nice situation already, it's not for you. Furthermore, you shouldn't read this book if you don't want to go beyond your comfort zone or if you don't want to try new things. Are you afraid of failing? If your answer is yes, you know what I'll tell you: not for you.

To achieve your goal, you have to want it and be willing to fail if necessary. I have bad news for you: it's a never-ending journey. You'll constantly have to work on your brand. But it's a journey that will make every day of your life better. In the end, who doesn't want to wake up on a weekday and be happy because he likes his job? Personally, it's the best thing that has ever happened to me. I don't hate Mondays anymore.

I Don't Have Time

In many of the talks I've presented on this topic, the first response from an audience member has been "I don't have time." And: "It all sounds beautiful, with bells and unicorns and it would be something amazing for me to do, but I don't have time."

I get it. We all have busy lives: family, friends, a job, and time to relax. The beauty of personal branding is that it shouldn't take you much time once you define what your brand will be. You should be able to integrate many aspects of it into your job, or at least figure out a way to start doing so. I'm a huge fan of being efficient and emphasizing impact: you'll focus only on what is important to achieve your goal and what will have an impact. The only exception I can think of is if your goal is not related at all to what you're actually doing—like you are thinking of going in a totally different direction in a different industry. But I'm not going to lie to you, either. Personal branding won't happen by magic. If you don't want to dedicate the time to improve your life and your career, it won't happen by itself.

Let the Fun Begin

I'm a huge believer that everything you do in life should be fun. I consider this book to be a program that guides you from the idea of reaching your goals to the result of creating a personal brand that will help you achieve them. For the duration of this program, I have only one rule (two, if we consider that I want you to challenge me on everything): have fun. As seriously as you take your career, if you get no pleasure from working on your personal brand, it isn't worth it—and more important, it won't work. Remember, the real foundation of your goal is probably to be happier in life, because of a new position, more money, a bigger network, and so on. Did you ever succeed at something you didn't like?

Chapter 1 | Personal What?

People often say that I repeat myself, and this book will be no exception. There are concepts that are so important that they are worth a couple more words in this book. So again, keep in mind that your personal brand is about you and every aspect of you that has forged who you are. It's not about being as intense as one of those big brands we all know, but it's still about marketing yourself: it's about being a linchpin—becoming that piece of the puzzle that you can't remove and being indispensable in your industry with your expertise.

Let the fun begin!

CHAPTER 2

I'm Not a Rock Star

So Why Should I Care?

> *Here's to the crazy ones. The misfits. The rebels. The troublemakers. The round pegs in the square holes. The ones who see things differently ... they change things. They push the human race forward. And while some may see them as the crazy ones, we see genius.*
>
> —Apple's "Think Different" ad campaign

As a developer, your job is to create software, right? So why should you care about your personal branding? You're not an actor or a rock star. In this chapter, I focus on why you should care about your personal brand. I discuss the benefits of thinking about yourself and your career as a brand. I also share some examples of successful people who have built their brands, along with my own experience. Throughout this book, you'll read testimonials from personalities in the IT world that highlight their experience and what they think about personal branding.

Maybe you bought this book out of curiosity, and you're not sure if it's the right book for you. Maybe someone gave you a copy (be sure to thank them), and you're not sure it will be relevant. Or maybe you're already aware of the benefits this book could have on your life. No matter how you came to it, you have already made the first step. You'll succeed only if you believe in the importance of personal branding. Even if you're already sold on the value of branding, I suggest you not skip this chapter. The more you know about the benefits of personal branding, the more you'll take action and make it happen.

Chapter 2 | I'm Not a Rock Star

No matter if you're creating websites, mobile applications, or standalone software, whether you're an employee or a freelancer, use open-source or proprietary technology, code in JavaScript, Python, C#, CSS, Ruby, Java, Rust, HTML or C++—at the end of the day, branding your career will help you. In fact, no matter what job you do—from waitress to accountant in a multinational firm—branding is something you should think about. Branding is critical in today's world. You can't just be an average developer. You need to differentiate yourself and achieve visibility. If you don't jump on the train right now, someone else will do it.

You Are Not Indispensable

You need to face the truth: you are not indispensable. Let me write it again: *You are not indispensable.*

We don't live in a world where employers can only choose from a limited base of people. With the Internet, my company can hire a developer anywhere in the world. Maybe your company isn't about remote working yet, but more employers in the industry are embracing this new way of working. People anywhere can easily communicate with each other. Think about tools like FaceTime, Skype, IRC, GoToMeeting, Google Hangouts, and more. My team is all across the world: in the United States, Canada, Sweden, and the United Kingdom. Even if people live in the same country or state, they're often not in the same city. Do we have trouble working together? Not at all. Of course, we like to get together once in a while, but we work 90 percent of the time in different locations. When Mozilla hired me, they only had two criteria about my location: I had to have a good Internet connection and not live too far from an airport.

Maybe you're your own boss. Even as a freelancer, you need to keep this in mind: your customers can find new partners at any moment, from anywhere in the world. Even if it's still true that most people prefer to work with someone they can meet face to face, it's becoming less and less true nowadays. Recently, I needed a designer to make a logo and found one who understood what I had in mind. I never met her face to face—she lives in Amsterdam. She was able to properly communicate by the Internet, and she did an amazing design job.

You may tell me you don't have to worry because you have a good diploma or degree. I'm not here to share my opinion of the educational system, but let's face it, university degrees have less impact than they used to. It may differ in other cultures, but it's true from what I'm seeing in North America at least. A degree helps you in the beginning, when you don't have a lot of experience. But after a year or two, it becomes more about what you have done and what you can do than which piece of paper you have.

There are many ways to prove yourself these days. A developer can showcase experience and expertise by showing code examples on GitHub. Since I finished school more than 10 years ago, I've had four different jobs, along with a couple of customers when I was a freelancer. Except for my first job, none of those employers or customers asked about my education. They wanted to know what I was capable of.

Let me share with you another slice of life. A couple years ago, I was working as a developer in a small company. For different, nonrelated reasons many employees decided to quit within the space of three to four months. Some wanted to go back to school, one wanted to work in a different industry, another found a new challenge somewhere else. It wasn't intentional on their behalf, but it became a huge issue. How could this company continue to be successful when the longtime employees were leaving? Many thought it would be the end for the company. But it wasn't. It was probably not an easy moment for the owner and the other employees, but they survived and are stronger now than they were. We were not indispensable.

No Job Is Secure

Here's a lesson I learned some years ago: no job is secure. You're doing a good job, and the company seems to be doing fine. Maybe now everything is good, but things can change. Let me tell you a small story about my career (I'm sure you understand now why I'm a public speaker—I like to share stories with others.)

Several years ago, I was working at a startup, and the company was doing well, or at least that's what I thought. I even had a discussion with my boss about becoming a more active member of the company and a partner instead of just an employee. Overall, I was happy with my job, and we were working on an amazing product. Unfortunately, the product didn't sell quickly enough. Now instead of talking about how I could become a partner, we were talking about me losing my job. Maybe I was naive, but I never saw it coming. Suddenly I had to think about my future and what I could do to support myself.

Of course, that may never happen to you. I hope it doesn't. But unless if you find a way to travel to the future and back, there's no way to know. Even if you work in a big company, what would happen if it decided to stop working on the product you own? What would happen if it eliminated your entire department? Sadly, this has happened to some of my friends, and possibly some of yours too.

Note Be ready. You never know when the situation will change, either because of your choices or because of situations beyond your control.

New Opportunities Ahead

I'm a positive person, so let's focus on something more fun. Let's think about not losing your job and liking what you do. Maybe there's a next step you would like to take in the career type you already have. For myself, I was a developer who liked his job, but I discovered the technical evangelist type of job, and I knew that was what I wanted to do from then on. It's not that I didn't like to code all day. I just wanted to do something new in the industry I liked so much. I believe there's always a way to improve your situation. Even now, when I love my job so much, I know what I can do to improve it and what will be my next step.

Maybe there's a new job in your industry that didn't exist before, or you didn't know about it when you started your career. Maybe there's a new position inside your company with challenges you would like to take on. Or maybe there's a company you've always dreamed about working for. Your goal could also be to reach the next level in your current role, moving from junior to senior. No matter what you want to improve in your career, personal branding will help you.

Thinking Beyond Yourself

Funnily enough, personal branding isn't just about you. The main focus of thinking about yourself as a brand *is* you, of course. The goal is to improve your situation and reach new goals, but it's not just selfish. By branding yourself, you'll have an impact on others' lives, and more than you think.

Ever hear the expression *dumbed down*? You may have seen this at school when the level to pass an exam was lowered so more students could pass their tests, a process called *leveling*. Dumbed down isn't the only direction for leveling, and what I'm proposing to you is to change the trend, as I firmly believe you can also level by the top. Did you ever notice that you don't get better if you're the most knowledgeable person in the room? What happens if you're suddenly surrounded by people who are more brilliant than you (at least with regard to a specific task)? You learn from them. You want to become better, to surpass them. You'll improve your skills in that situation. By being that person, you will help others—you'll be leveling by the top. This is why I think that by working on your personal brand, you'll help others achieve their goals, too.

Personal branding by itself won't make you more happy with your life, but the results of it may do the trick. If you like what you do for a living and wake up in the morning happy to go to work, personal branding will make a difference—in your life and the lives of others. If you're happier, your friends, your spouse, your kids, even your cats will be even happier. Happiness is contagious.

I also believe in leading by example. If you try to go the extra mile, if you believe in the power of personal branding, others around you will, too. By working on your brand, you'll also improve your skills, have a bigger impact, and get more visibility. Your company, customers, co-workers, and anyone gravitating around your day-to-day job will benefit from it.

Maslow's Hierarchy of Needs

Look at the pyramid shown in Figure 2-1. Perhaps you saw it in one of your college philosophy or psychology courses. Personal branding is often seen as something trivial, but it's not. It's more important than you think, and here's the proof: I'm using a well-known theory to prove it!

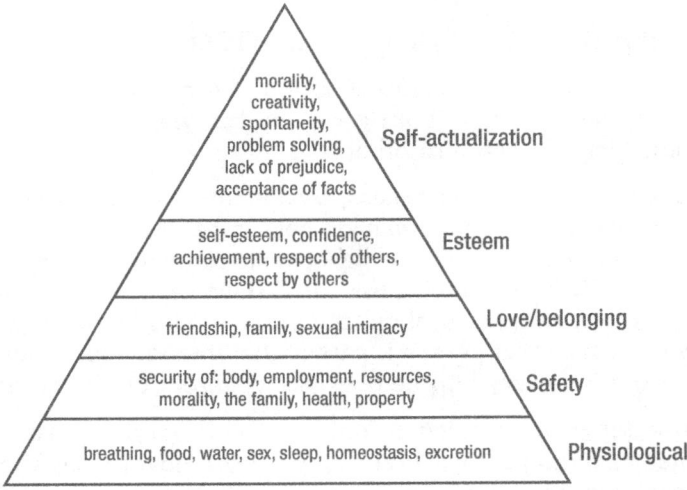

Figure 2-1. Maslow's hierarchy of needs

Figure 2-1 represents the hierarchy of needs proposed more than 70 years ago by the American psychologist Abraham Maslow. I leave to you the responsibility of most of these needs, but let's focus on certain items and categories. Let's start with security of employment in the Safety category. I told you that no one is indispensable, but by working on your personal brand, you can make yourself harder to replace. By doing so, it will be easier for you to get and keep a job you like. It's obvious that by getting paid to do a specific task, it will be easier to buy food, get a roof over your head, and raise a family.

If your sole reason for building your brand is notoriety, you're doing it for the wrong reasons. Many people would like to be a celebrity, but if you have no real passion for what you do, or worse, don't even like it, then you're setting yourself up for failure. I'm not from the entertainment industry, but I'm pretty sure that no actor is successful without loving what he or she does. There's nothing wrong with wanting more fame. Like any human being, you want recognition from your peers and respect from others. You also want to be confident about yourself and what you do, and no matter what, you should have healthy self-esteem. By improving yourself and your brand, you'll achieve new things you'll be proud of. Not only that, you'll harvest some of the good stuff at the top of Maslow's pyramid: esteem and self-actualization.

The needs at the top of the pyramid are there for a reason: they aren't the most important criteria to have for a healthy life. If you're reading this book, you're one of the lucky people whose priority is not finding food to eat tomorrow. Only when you've fulfilled most of your basic needs can you aim for a higher peak.

You Are Already Being Branded

Whether or not you're conscious of it, you already have a personal brand. People already define you, in both good and bad ways, and who you are is already something of a brand to others.

Think about one of your colleagues, perhaps the one you work with most closely. How would you define him or her? Is he always late to meetings? Always going the extra mile to give higher value to the client? Always creating bugs while committing something in your GitHub repository? Maybe it's the person who knows everything about the programming language you're using. Every way you define that person is part of their brand. Your co-worker may not be realize it, but everything he does has an impact on their brand.

It's the same for you. It's called an opinion—and everybody has an opinion about someone. With personal branding, you learn how to help those people have the *right* opinion about you. It's not about manipulating people or being anything other than yourself. It's about improving your brand and making it stronger.

Fighting the Impostor Syndrome

Maybe you don't want to be a rock star developer or differentiate from others. Maybe you just want to do your job. (I get it. I'm like that sometimes.) But there's a difference between doing your job and doing a *great* job. So don't become a victim of the impostor syndrome. You may feel like an impostor while working on your brand. Every successful person I know has this syndrome: you think you got where you are by sheer luck. The truth is, it's not about luck. You worked hard to be where you are right now. Even if you're not successful yet, you deserve to be. Don't you have goals? Don't you want to reach the next step? You deserve it as much as anyone else does.

Maybe someone else already has a strong personal brand like the one you want. Do you give up on applying to a job because other developers are applying? If only one expert per topic existed, life would be boring. Each brand, no matter how similar they may look, is different. Like humans, every brand is unique. You have a special approach to your expertise, your brand. You think differently. Your network is one of a kind. Where you live is special. There are many ways to differentiate yourself from the crowd, and I'll show you how.

A Personal Story: Building My Own Brand

This book isn't about me, and that's a good thing for you. But I'm going to tell you why I started caring about personal branding.

It started more than five years ago. I was working in a small startup, building web and mobile applications, and I lost my job. I thought it was a good opportunity to think about my career and not just jump to the next job automatically. I wanted to think about what I was doing and where I wanted to go next. Even though it was bad news, I saw it as an opportunity—a chance to start my own business and become a freelancer. So I did that. But I also wanted to be a technical evangelist. I have a skill that few developers have: I'm social. I'd already had the pleasure of meeting some technical evangelists at events I had attended. Meeting them opened my eyes to a new role, a new possibility for me.

Note What exactly is a technical evangelist? Someone who gives love to developers. I'm a spokesperson, helping developers who are successful with our platform. I'm also the link between the product team and the developers—I gather valuable feedback. My day-to-day job runs the gamut from presenting at conferences or workshops to coding, writing, mentoring, and more. It's a lovely mix of technical skills with social ones. In the end, it's a bit more complex than that, but basically I get paid to share my passion for technology with other developers.

I had no experience as a technical evangelist. As a developer, I only knew the technical side, and frankly, that's the easy part. The technical stuff is super important of course, but I found it easier to learn the technical skills and languages than to develop personality skills. So I decided to build the personality skills I was missing and create the experience I needed to become a technical evangelist: public speaking, organizing events, creating technical blog posts, and sharing more about the IT industry. I was starting my own business, so this wasn't a short-term plan. I tried to find something that would make sense for my business and help me get paid to be a technical evangelist. At that point, I didn't know I was starting to build my brand, but that's what I was doing.

I made a list of skills and experience I needed. I decided to focus on the fact that I'm a doer, someone who makes things happen. So I started to assist at more conferences and user groups. I started to give talks, too, to show people that I was able to be a technical evangelist and share my expertise and passion with others. I started to network a lot more: meeting new people, going to networking events, and taking my social media presence to the next level. I began to blog a lot more professionally—again, to show my expertise or at least my way of thinking. Last but not least, with the help of some amazing people, I started a festival in Montreal called GeekFest Montreal. It wasn't a conference or even something related directly to IT. It was a festival for geeks, a culture I was passionate about and part of. It showed people my leadership and helped me grow my visibility and my network. Most important, it made me switch from being a talker to a doer.

All these activities proved to other people and myself that I had the personality to be a technical evangelist. I had the technical skills, because I had been a developer. I was able to speak in front of an audience, because I had to do that for conferences. I was responsible, social, passionate, and a doer and I had a great network. You get the point: I made a decision to acquire the soft skills that I didn't have and prove to the world I was the man to do this job. A couple months after I started as a freelancer, Microsoft approached me for a technical evangelist role. There's no denying that having a company like Microsoft offer you the role you are dreaming of is quite an achievement.

For a little less than three years, I was talking about open source at Microsoft as a technical evangelist. I was traveling all across Canada, presenting at conferences, and helping developers be successful on our platform. Today, as a senior technical evangelist at Mozilla, I'm traveling all over the world to share the love about web technologies like HTML and Firefox OS.

By building my brand, I went from an average developer in a small shop in Montreal to a technical evangelist speaking worldwide. I'm not saying it's bad to be a developer in a small shop in Montreal. I just wasn't the best developer out there; I was average. I had other expectations for my career at that point. I want to be very clear on that point: being an evangelist isn't better than being a developer. It was better for *me*, though, for what I wanted to do for a living. I wanted to organize events, speak at conferences, help other developers, share my passion, and travel. Now that stuff is the main part of my job.

Even in this book itself, I'm sharing my passion and beliefs in personal branding because I want you to get all the benefits out of it, too. It's not a secret I want to keep: I want more people to know about the power of personal branding.

Nothing Will Happen by Magic

Unless you live in Harry Potter's world, nothing happens by magic. Sorry, but you need to work to achieve your goals. Do you want that promotion? Is your next step to move up a level? As with everything in life, you need to make it happen. I don't believe in luck. I'm making my own luck, and it's the same for my career. I know countless people who don't like their jobs, but do nothing about it. They expect that someone, somewhere, someday will offer them their dream job. That may happen, but I wouldn't wait for it. Personal branding can help you create your own luck, approach your end goals, and make them a reality.

Start Now

We all should have started thinking about personal branding from the very beginning of our careers, but it's never too late to get started. Like when people lose their jobs—I'm always amazed when a developer tells me he's updating his LinkedIn profile and networking because he just lost his job. It's a bit too late. He should have been continuously updating his LinkedIn profile and résumé all along. He should have been networking back when he didn't *need* a job.

I want you to be proactive, not reactive. Your personal brand is not something you'll build in one day. It will be a long (okay, not so long) but worthwhile journey.

So, start now, change things, and let's be the *crazy* ones.

CHAPTER 3

Me, Myself, and I

The Who

Become who you are!

—Friedrich Nietzsche, from *Thus Spake Zarathustra*

As mentioned, I'll share with you some bits of knowledge from others in the technology industry. These are people I admire, who all have one point in common: personal branding has been useful for them. It helped them reach the point in their careers where they are now.

My friend, coworker, and mentor Christian Heilmann is one of the most well-known technical evangelists in the web industry. I asked Christian whether he thinks personal branding is important for a developer, and why:

> *It is more important than one thinks as a developer. The biggest issue is that it feels icky. As a developer, you look up to other developers for what they did, not how they sell themselves. Even worse, people who tell the world how amazing they are appear as frauds to us. The issue is that other developers are not likely to hire you or get you new contracts. We cannot expect people to come into our world and find out who is who. People don't know what makes us better developers, which is why we need to be visible in a different way. And this is where personal branding comes in. Become known as a helpful techie and dare to keep up with current affairs and offer your thoughts on them, and you'll show up on people's radar.*

Christian has a strong brand: he is a well-known speaker in the industry, doing many conferences a year, and is seen as a leader on new technology. Because of that, I asked him how thinking about himself as a brand (consciously or not) helped him in his career:

> It helped me to make the switch from engineer to spokesperson. Our market is still broken: as a technical person, you have only a few levels to advance inside a company. Higher paid jobs with more responsibility also demand different degrees or even MBAs. I did not want to go into upper management but instead wanted to keep being excited about technology and work on it. Thus, becoming known as an engineer that is available to communicate and connect you with others helped me out of this dilemma.

Chris is an endless source of insight when it comes to the tech industry.[1] I asked him to share some advice about using personal branding to reach the next goal in your career.

> Be visible, but don't steal other people's thunder. Always attribute where attribution is due and tell people when you advocate their work for them. Our market is small and you will always cross paths with former colleagues in the future. Don't burn bridges. On the other hand, be bold when you need to be. A lot of tech became a reality because people dared to tell people about it without listing all its faults at the same time.

You can follow Christian on Twitter (his handle is codepo8) and check out his blog (www.christianheilmann.com), which is full of technology awesomeness. With those words of wisdom, let's move to the core topic of this chapter: yourself!

Who Are You?

Chapter 1 talked a little about what guides your personal branding. Of course, this is only one part of the puzzle. Chapter 2 was a way to prove to yourself that thinking about yourself as a brand is important. The next chapters go into more detail on every aspect of personal branding and how to use it to achieve your goals. I start with the first pillar of personal branding: the *who*.

Who are you? This question is both simple and complex. Who you are will be the foundation of your brand. We are talking about personal branding here, after all. You are the first thing you need to define. In this chapter, you will take the time to define who you are. Think of it as an opportunity to do some introspection. As I get older, I know myself more and more. I've even started to take personality tests online and in books: they help me confirm what I think about myself. Personal branding is built on who you are, so take the time you need to answer the personality questions included later in this chapter.

Be Authentic

No matter the situation, always stay yourself. It's super important that the brand you build is based on the truth. You'll be like a WYSIWYG editor: what people see is what they will get.

Of course, nobody wants to work with a liar. Nobody wants to hire someone who amplifies the facts, and nobody wants to work with someone who has two faces. It's a lot easier to work on your brand if you don't have to invent stuff or pretend to be someone you are not. Isn't it just easier to be yourself? On top of that, keep in mind that the truth will always come out sooner or later.

It's not just about what you say. It's also how you act, what you like, what you dislike, how you think, how you dress, and so on. Every little aspect that is part of you needs to be ... you. Of course, it's not always easy, but in the end, it will pay off. I learned that you cannot please everyone, and I stopped trying to do it. One of the decisions I made was to stop dressing like the industry wanted me to dress: dress pants and a button-down shirt. Most of my time was spent in front of a computer creating software. I was pretty sure that wearing jeans didn't make me less competent, even when I was with customers. I figured you can't judge a book by its cover, so I decided to verify that old saying by wearing running shoes, jeans, and a geeky T-shirt all the time. As you might suspect, I was wrong: people *do* judge books by their covers! It was not a real test, because I knew what would happen. People who didn't know me judged me as someone less serious, less responsible, and even less competent in my work. But it was okay because I wanted to stay true to myself. Those clothes were representing me, and it was in them that I was most comfortable. So don't hide your tattoos or piercings: they will always be there, so your future manager should be okay with them. Can't live without your baseball cap? Feel free to keep it on inside the office if there are no rules against it. You like to listen to music while coding? Keep doing it! Be clear to your coworkers that just because you have headphones on doesn't mean you are not a team player or are unavailable to them. For any attribute or way of doing things you have, keep it, and stay yourself!

I'm doing a very interesting little experiment. I have a lot of visibility because I do public speaking. Every time I go on stage, meet a new person, or talk to a potential partner, their perception of me starts lower than it normally would for a first contact. Everyone says the first impression is the most important and that you only have a brief amount of time to make a good impression. I don't think I'm making a bad impression, but according to business protocol, it's not the one I should be making. That puts it all on me to change the inaccurate idea people immediately form and win their hearts and minds.

It's a double-edged sword: I may not have time to change the perceptions of some people, and they'll end up keeping their false idea of who I am. But if you give me the time to let you know that I'm more than this pair of jeans, the effect will be doubled! Remember that speaker you thought would do a poor job at a conference or that new coworker you thought you wouldn't want to work with? What happened when they turned out to be amazing? A huge surprise for you, and a big change in your opinion. Your opinion of them probably ended up higher than if it had been better in the beginning. I use this "disadvantage" to my advantage—by staying myself. Remember those tattoos I mentioned? You shouldn't hide them, as they're now part of you. But keep in mind that the person doing the interview for an amazing new gig you want may not appreciate them. As I said, it's a double-edged sword, but you can use the element of surprise to your advantage. What if the new coworker judges you as incompetent because you are full of piercings? They may be surprised and may regret having judging you so quickly.

I remember one social media presentation I did. It's one of my passions, and not everybody was a social media expert at the time I gave the presentation, at a conference for engineers. Social media was not something that this group of engineers knew about, so it was an interesting challenge. I remember the scene: *everybody* was in a suit and was a lot older than I. They had been in the job market for way longer than I had—some even before I was born.

At that time, I was not totally into the "being yourself" philosophy when it came to my clothes, so I had on a button-down shirt, and guess what? That shirt was outside of the pants, and it was not what you could call dress wear—more like what a lumberjack would wear. With my jeans, shaved head, and goatee, I went on stage. I'll always remember the look on their faces. Something like, "What the fudge? We'll waste the next hour with this guy . . ." I didn't fit into that crowd at all. They all judged me, of course, without knowing me. The only one in the room who was proud of seeing me on the stage was the organizer.

I did my presentation, and it went (for them) surprisingly well. I got a lot of amazing questions and interest from that crowd and received a lot of praise during the break after my talk. Another speaker was a specialist in corporate images for businessmen and -women. She told me (I'm paraphrasing): "When I saw you in front, I was discouraged and was sure I was going to waste my time. I could not have been more wrong. You were interesting, energetic, well prepared, and you knew your subject. I learned a lot, and it was one of the best talks of the day. You are such a persona." See what happened? Her expectation was low when she saw me. After my talk, she was so pleasantly surprised that her reaction went the other way and smashed through the roof.

Be authentic. It pays to be yourself in every situation. Keep that in mind for the rest of this chapter, the book, and your entire life.

Past, Present, and Future

Who you are is also built on your past and your future—who you were and who you want to be. Every action, good or bad, has helped forge who you are right now, and who you will be in the future. You learn from what you did, and also from what you didn't do.

Recently I was presenting to students at my alma mater, Herzing College. My goal was to help them differentiate themselves not just from other students in their class but also from other students elsewhere, and from other people in the industry. In the end, it was a quick introduction to personal branding for developers, as all those students were going to graduate and become developers, too. Part of my talk was about contributing to open-source projects (a topic I come back to later in the book). One student asked me if I contributed to open-source projects when I started in the IT industry. My answer was no, but since then I've realized how important it is and I know it would have helped me along the way (for many reasons). Look at me now: I work to promote an open-source project.

You must take into account who you want to be and what you would like to change about you. I'm not talking about being someone else—never be someone else.

What Is Your Elevator Pitch?

Are you on Twitter? After blogs, Twitter is one of my preferred social media. I like its simplicity, and I cherish those 140 characters. I used to hate that limitation when I started to tweet in 2008. Today, I think it's important to know how to express yourself in a few words. It helps you clarify your thoughts.

I would like you to define yourself in a tweet, using 140 characters. No cheating! You can use fewer than that or finish with the last character being the 140th, but no more. I am asking you to do this because you need a personal elevator pitch. In the business world, an *elevator pitch* is a summary used to define your value proposition. The idea is that if you are in an elevator with someone, and only have a couple of seconds to introduce yourself with maximum impact, what would you say? Having an elevator pitch is important, because networking will be a key part of building your brand and helping yourself reach the next goal. Try to include everything that is important to know about you—personal traits, hobbies, your career, the programming languages you know, and so on. Assume that the person receiving your pitch knows your jargon. There are no limitations on what defines you. After all, you are the one who know you best.

Don't know where to start? Here's my elevator pitch. (I even got it down to 136 characters, so efficient!):

> Sr. technical evangelist at Mozilla, web lover, T-shirt geek, music aficionado, public speaker, social beast, blogger, doing epic shit!

It's a pitch I've been using for a while. I've refined it quite a bit. Yours may be quite different. For the sake of this exercise, let me unpack it.

- **Sr. technical evangelist at Mozilla:** Why have my job as the first item? My work is super important. I need to do something I like. Think about it: you spend more time at the office than with your friends and family. It's also something I'm proud of. Being an evangelist is unusual, too, so it's an amazing ice breaker for any conversation. Most people are probably more comfortable with non-personal stuff, so I think it's a good idea to start my elevator pitch with something professional. I'm also happy to be at Mozilla. It's more than a company to me. I associate myself with our mission, and I'm proud to work there. Same goes for you if your job is important to you. You don't have to be as specific as I was: you can just say *developer*. You don't even have to add a job type in your elevator pitch, but since you will use it professionally, I feel that it makes sense.

- **Web lover:** You would probably guess that I like the web, since the first item in that list is that I'm working at Mozilla. No matter my job, I feel the desire to reiterate my fondness for the web because it's important to me. I like the web as a web developer and as a user, so it's not just my job. So let's be bold and make a statement here: I love the web. It's always a matter of choice, and you don't have to have a statement like this, but feel free to add what you love. The more precise you are, the more impact your pitch will have.

- **T-shirt geek:** Everything that makes you who you are, even your clothes, can be part of your brand. T-shirts are clearly part of my personal brand, as I'm always wearing geek or funny T-shirts. It's to the point that people who have seen me are always on the lookout for what will be my next shirt. I even have people stop me at conferences to see which one I'm wearing and are happy to discover a new one or disappointed if it's one they already saw. People expect me to wear a cool T-shirt no matter where I go. I even had to start a blog series about my T-shirts because people often ask me where I bought them, so I tell them. Once I posted a picture of me wearing a dress shirt at an event—it was the obligatory dress code for all working at our booth, and many comments expressed surprise that I was not wearing a T-shirt. Of course, for you, it may not be your clothes that differentiate you: it could be your hairstyle, funky glasses, or anything else. Whatever that is, take this opportunity to put it at the front of your one-liner.

- **Music aficionado:** This one is a part of me that many people do not know that much about. A huge music fan, I listen to music every day. This trait is not part of who I want to be, as I'm already a music aficionado, but part of who I already am that I would like to push out a little more. As the master of my brand, I can direct it in the sense I want. Now that people know a little more about my music tastes, they have started suggesting good albums to buy or artists to listen to. It's a good way to show people that I'm not just about what I do for living, but have other passions. You don't have to go personal, but as you probably would in job interviews, it's never bad to show that you have passions other than work. Share what you love. It's also an opportunity to give visibility to some projects you have.

- **Public speaker:** If you know what a technical evangelist is, you know it involves public speaking, but again, I want to emphasize that this is something important to me. I like to share my passion and expertise with others. I even do it outside of my job: I accept personal speaking gigs to talk about nontechnical topics, just for the fun of sharing some of my passion with others. In the past three years, I've done about 100 talks for conferences or user groups. I've also spoken in more than 10 countries in the past year. So it's part of who I am, and I want to highlight that. This can be a good subject for discussion. It may also help people remember me when they look for a speaker for their events and lead to new speaking opportunities! Everything you previously listed is part of you, what you do, and what you like, but do you have something else you are proud of you that you'd like to share? Think about differentiating yourself from others. Imagine that you are in a networking event and that the person you just introduced yourself to had said hi to 10 people before you: how will she remember you?

- **Social beast:** As I've said, I have a special personality trait that many developers do not have: I'm social. I like people. I like to be with people. People fascinate me. It's nearly unhealthy, but it's a critical part of who I am, so I want to showcase this personal aspect that helps make me unique. I also want to show people that I'm not just a usual social person. They can invite me to any event—I'll always be comfortable, even if I don't know anyone else. I will often sit down with people I don't know at a local bar. My friends may leave, but I want to make new connections before going home. It could be a good idea to share bits of your personality. You don't have to share everything, just what you think is important. You are an introvert, but have no problem talking one on one to people? It's the time to mention that because it may help the person you talk with understand you better. Maybe you are the kind of developers who always make people laugh around the water cooler. Why not share that with others? Better yet, show them by being fun and humorous. It's a nice personal trait!

- **Blogger:** Blogging is somewhat related to my job because it's part of my role right now, but that wasn't always so. Did I tell you that the line between working and having fun for me is fuzzy sometimes? I've been blogging since 2005. Even while blogging for Microsoft, and now for Mozilla, I would say that 99 percent of the posts I've published have been on my personal blog. I like to share with others, and the blog is an amazing tool for this. (We'll come back to this platform in future chapters, as it will be a key to add to your personal branding tool chest.) If you blog, consider putting it in your elevator pitch. You tweet like no one else? Add it. You know all the secrets behind Google+? Share it with others.

- **Doing epic shit:** Ah, my mantra, my life manifesto. What does it mean? Basically, doing amazing things. I'm trying to live every day of my life by thinking about it. I even put an exclamation mark in the end to emphasize this importance, and give it even more awesomeness. In the end, we only have a limited number of years to live, so why not make it worthwhile by doing epic things? I put it at the end of my elevator pitch because it sums up everything I do. It's also a summary of everything else that I was not able to fit in the limited number of characters.

That's it: the deconstruction of the tweet/elevator pitch that defines me, which I use when presenting myself. Even if it feels simple, there is a lot of information in this elevator pitch: some personal, some related to my day job, some obvious, some not. Keep in mind that it's not always possible to get in all the information at once. Your pitch is a good starter for a situation when you meet someone new: they want to know who you are and what you do in life.

Try it yourself right now. I won't read it (although if you want feedback, drop me a line at fharper@oocz.net). Try to be serious about this exercise, and more important, be honest with yourself. Write it in the lines below, and we'll use it later. Don't take too much time; it's a first draft. We're going to refine it.

___ ___ ___ ___ ___ ___ ___ ___ ___ ___ ___ ___ ___ ___
___ ___ ___ ___ ___ ___ ___ ___ ___ ___ ___ ___ ___ ___
___ ___ ___ ___ ___ ___ ___ ___ ___ ___ ___ ___ ___ ___
___ ___ ___ ___ ___ ___ ___ ___ ___ ___ ___ ___ ___ ___
___ ___ ___ ___ ___ ___ ___ ___ ___ ___ ___ ___ ___ ___
___ ___ ___ ___ ___ ___ ___ ___ ___ ___ ___ ___ ___ ___
___ ___ ___ ___ ___ ___ ___ ___ ___ ___ ___ ___ ___ ___
___ ___ ___ ___ ___ ___ ___ ___ ___

You can always refine your elevator pitch, of course, even long after you read this book. It's a picture in time, but it can and should evolve. By the end of this chapter, you'll see that it may be changing already from what you'll learn or confirm about yourself.

Scratching the Surface Is Not Enough

Now that you have your elevator pitch, let's dig deeper. Let's think about who you are in a more exhaustive way. You'll use your pitch to define where you want to go, what you want to improve, and what your goal is.

Unlike the first version of your elevator pitch, you won't write down the revised version in this book. Use software or pen and paper instead. The following exercise is incredibly useful, but it's not something you need to keep after you refine your elevator pitch.

I want you to answer the following questions—at least those that make sense for you—with a small sentence or just a few words. Don't overthink this, and there is no question more important than another one. This exercise should help define what is most important to you.

Chapter 3 | Me, Myself, and I

1. What are your strengths?
2. What are your weaknesses?
3. How do you normally dress?
4. What is your work experience?
5. What are you proudest of?
6. What foods do you like?
7. What kind of music do you like?
8. What is your marital/family status?
9. Do you like to travel?
10. What are your passions?
11. What are your hobbies?
12. Is religion important for you?
13. Do you have pets?
14. What are your favorite websites?
15. What is important to you in life?
16. What is not important for you?
17. What makes you happy?
18. What makes you sad?
19. What makes you mad?
20. What superpower would you like to have (or already have)?

I'll stop there, because I would be able to fill many pages with similar questions, but you get the point. These are all about defining yourself a bit more with personal answers. Feel free to add questions you think might be important to you. Go crazy—and go ahead and do those online quizzes about yourself or the ones you find in magazines. Feel free to add any other words, sentences, or anything that will give more meat to the things that describe yourself. You may think that I should have told you to do this before your elevator pitch, but bear with me, it's better to do it now.

You'll use those answers to help you define what your personal brand will be.

How Others See You

As mentioned in Chapter 1, a big part of your personal brand is how people see you—what they perceive from you. Sometimes it seems we are living in a world where we want to please people so much that we tend to forget about ourselves, what we like, and who we are. Let me tell you a quick story.

When I was a freelancer, as you may remember, I offered my services as a web and mobile developer. It's where I got some of my experience, and it's one the work I enjoyed the most. My offer on the mobile side was for the following platforms: Blackberry, Windows Mobile, and iPhone. You can tell I'm not that young because some of these are not popular anymore, and some don't even exist today. Android was a rising star, but not enough to add it to my already (too) long list of services. Actually, I had experience building for Blackberry and Windows Mobile, but not for iPhone. I needed to offer iPhone to be successful, because so many companies were looking to outsource the development of their revolutionary iPhone applications.

I learn quickly and on my own. I offered iPhone development, knowing that I had no experience. When talking with prospects, I was totally transparent about that. They would have a quality app, because I had experience with mobile development, but they would not pay for my learning curve of developing for Apple. I even gave a rebate to my first customer who wanted an iPhone app.

At that time, my network was growing because of my involvement in the industry at the networking events I participated in. People started sending me leads, which is invaluable when you start your own company. Their conversations with potential customers went something like this: "I know this guy, Fred. You should talk to him. He's offering iPhone app development, and he is amazing, professional, and will deliver you a quality app." I was flattered by their way of introducing me, but it was weird. Most of the people who introduced me to their contacts had never seen one of my apps. I didn't even have an iPhone app to show anybody. Most of the people who introduced me as a good developer had never worked with me!

The truth is, their perception was that I was professional and I was going to do a good job of creating an iPhone app. They trusted me enough to put their credibility on the table for me. It was all about their perception. I could have been the worst programmer in the world, but they were still sending me leads—based not on what they knew, but on what they thought they knew.

How others see you is extremely important. It's why I want you to do another exercise: whether by creating a blog post, publishing a status on Facebook, writing a tweet, or asking verbally, ask your network, *How do you see me, and what kind of person do you think I am?* Don't ask just your closest friends. Do it at large: include friends, family, coworkers, and people that know you only online. You may be surprised by the answers you'll get. It may solidify what you thought about yourself, or it may provide new insights about yourself and how people see you that could be totally different from what you had in mind. You may hear things that makes sense but never occurred to you before.

While we wait for the answers from your network, let me sneak in another story. Recently, I was doing a presentation to a user group I founded. The organizer introduced me to the audience as a serial entrepreneur. At first, I was surprised, because we use the term *entrepreneur* too often to mean someone who has built a business. I had only built one, and it did not exist for very long. Then I realized what he had in mind: someone who always does stuff, taking ideas and making them reality. I had never thought about myself as a *serial* entrepreneur, but I realized I had started many successful things: a festival, a user group, a conference, a networking group, and more. He had defined me by something that was true but had never crossed my mind.

It should take too long to get some answers; after all, we live in a world of instantaneity. What feedback did you get? Was it what you were expecting? Was it good? Was it surprising? Did it make you think differently about yourself? Keep those answers in mind, along with your answers to the earlier questions. They will prove useful soon.

Remember: you already have a brand! That's why it's important to be proactive and manage it yourself instead of letting others manage it for you.

Focus on Your Strengths

I'm a big believer in self-improvement. There are many ways to do this. You can try to be better at a specific task or activity you are not currently good at. You can try to change a personality trait you do not like about yourself. You can learn to be more effective, efficient, or productive. You can try to get the most out of what you are doing by focusing on the impact you can have. Improvement is about more than building up your weaknesses. We all want to be better humans, citizens, and employees, and improvement requires a lot of time and effort. That's time you can use to improve your *strengths* and reach the next level. I'm not saying you shouldn't try to work on your weakness, but most of your time should be spent focusing on your strengths: doing so creates more impact.

A good guideline is to use 80 percent of your self-development time improving something you are already good at. For the other 20 percent, work on your weaknesses. Don't put too much on your plate. I would say work no more than one weakness and two strengths at a time. That's the guidance I've used these past couple of years, and it's working well.

I'm prioritizing my time to have more impact: that is one of my weaknesses. I want to do stuff that matters more and that will help me reach my goal faster. I have so many interests and ideas and know so many people that it's not always easy to manage my time efficiently and effectively. That's something I want to improve. On the positive side, I focus on maximizing two of my strengths: my social capabilities and my facility for sharing my passion with others.

For example, instead of always hanging with the same people at a networking event, I try to talk to people I do not know so I can grow my network. Your network is so critical that you should always be working on it. I devote an entire chapter to this topic, in fact. I'm also working to improve my ability to share passion easily, by presenting at conferences, writing blog posts, or finding some other way. Making a bigger impact is one of my themes. What are the other ways I can improve how I share my passion about technology? By reaching more people and helping more people become web literate. I started recording myself when presenting, and afterward I upload the video online and reach a lot more people than just the attendees who were in the room. I also upload my slides. (I discuss these and other tricks later in the book.)

One of the best books about finding what your strengths are and working on them is *Strength Finder 2.0* by Tom Rath (Gallup Press, 2007). I highly recommend reading it (after this book, of course) and doing the exercises.

What Differentiates You from Others?

It would be boring to live in a world where everybody was the same. You may have many of the same tastes as others, you may share abilities and wear the same clothes, but in the end, we are all unique. Keep in mind your answers to the questions posed earlier in this chapter and think about what differentiates you from your cohorts and from others in the industry. It may be something others have—it does not need to be exclusive to you. It might be something rare, something that sets you apart. Maybe you are more social than others, or you are more community driven. Anything that makes you different is something to highlight. Focus on the personal side. As you know now, it's about you, not just your skills. Write down what makes you special. We'll use it later to define your personal branding.

It's Only the Beginning

You may not realize it, but you've already started working on your brand. Further defining who you are—your strengths, weaknesses, how people see you, and what makes you different—are the foundations of the next chapter: what will be your brand.

Chapter 3 | Me, Myself, and I

You may be itching to create another version of your elevator pitch. You probably want to define your brand with more details right now, but be patient (I know, it's not always easy).

The goal of this chapter was to help you define yourself on the personal side and reflect on who you are right now and which aspects of yourself need some work. You will use this information to develop part of your brand. I'm not talking about sharing all personal aspects of your life in the online world or to coworkers. But whether you like it or not, your personality is a huge part of your brand.

CHAPTER 4

Defining Your Brand: Are You a Ninja, a Pirate, or a Rock Star?

The What

> *The only thing standing between you and your goal is the bullshit story you keep telling yourself as to why you can't achieve it.*
>
> —Jordan Belfort, author of *The Wolf of Wall Street*

Ninja, pirate, rock star—there are many ways to define good developers. I don't know about you, but I'm not a big fan of those terms. They are different ways of defining the same thing: a super developer. Your brand can help you reach the next level and be that super developer you always wanted to be.

This chapter aims to help you define your brand and manage it yourself as a professional, instead of letting others do it for you. It's all about how you differentiate yourself. Before going deeper, I'll share some knowledge from another successful developer.

In this chapter, I'm sharing the wisdom of Jonathan Leblanc, global head of developer evangelism at PayPal. I asked Jonathan whether he thinks personal branding is important for developers, and if so, why. Here is his answer:

> Really what we're talking about here is if thought leadership is important to being a developer—well, it is for anyone for whom being a developer is a way of life, not just a job. A typical open community will usually have 99% of the people using the product without contributing to it, and 1% that truly understand the vision of the project and can help guide its future. This might be a programming language, open source project, event, or anything else in the development realm. That 1% of people in a project are those that have decided that they wanted to be a part of something more than just themselves, becoming thought leaders in a community that they believe in. As you take on this thought leadership role, you will find that the exposure you get to many different visions and backgrounds will allow you to become a completely different, more well rounded, and overall better developer than you ever could have alone.

He couldn't be more right: working on your brand is about leadership (more on that in Chapter 5). Like me, Jonathan went from developer to evangelist. Let's see how personal branding helped him with his career:

> One of the most significant turning points in my career was when I started thinking about my interests and the impact that I wanted to have in the developer world. As I started to understand what I wanted from myself and my career, I took ownership of everything I possibly could to build up that personal brand for myself. As I truly started to engage as a thought leader in different spaces, I discovered that new opportunities opened themselves up to me to expand my knowledge and the work that I was doing in the open-source world. The connections, groups, and projects that I had a chance to engage with during this time became the foundation on which I built my entire career. The funny thing is, the areas I contribute to now, after years in the industry, have changed so significantly than where they started from—my brand matured as I did.

Here is what Jonathan Leblanc wants to share about reaching your goal using personal branding:

> There is one piece of advice that I would give for peers trying to discover their place in the developer community. When you find that thing that you really feel passionately about (for whatever reason), spend any chance to get to be a sponge as you learn everything you can about the community. If it's an open community, read message boards and bug logs to see how the community has grown, go to meetups and speak with other people in the community to learn from other experts in the field, watch videos and read tutorials to expand your knowledge about what's possible with the

> project. A difficult but valuable thing you can do is to learn from people who have completely contradictory opinions from your own. It's only when we start challenging our own notions about how something should be done, and questioning our own beliefs, that we can truly start helping to guide its future. Your voice will come in time, just be willing to get your hands dirty.

If you never meet Jonathan in person, you should take the time to talk to him next time you see him at a conference. Check out his website (www.jcleblanc.com)—there is always great content, such as slides and recordings of his presentations. And you can follow him on Twitter (jcleblanc). He is constantly sharing amazing ideas. He's my source for the latest JavaScript frameworks out there. I'm blessed to have such people in my network.

I was impatient to write this chapter because it's one of the most important parts of the book. It aims to help you define your goals and, of course, your brand. Your elevator pitch from Chapter 3 is going to be useful here. You'll use all the knowledge from all previous chapters to create your brand.

The Jordan Belfort epigraph at the beginning of this chapter says that the only thing standing between you and your dream is you. It's the same thing for your personal brand. At this point, the only thing preventing you from reaching your goal is you. So let's continue this journey!:

Defining Your Goal

It's one thing to realize that you need to control your brand, but it's another to take full control of it and use it to achieve your goals. This book is all about reaching the next level—but what *is* the next level? What do you want to achieve with your career? What is the next step for you? What is your end goal? You will never be successful with your personal brand if you don't know why you're doing it, so let's figure this out first.

Is It About Getting Your Dream Job?

Most often, when I'm talking about personal branding with developers, it's about them getting their dream job. They may like what they're doing, but there's always something better waiting for them. Actually, most of the time it *is* about people who don't like what they're doing for a living. Maybe they are not creating the software they like or they're not crazy about their colleagues, the projects they are working on, or the company.

When I started to be more conscious about my personal brand, it was my goal to go from developer to technical evangelist. That was my dream job. I was happy as a freelancer, but I knew what I wanted to do one day. So I made it my goal. What about you? Do you want to go from junior to a senior position? Are you looking to change to a new role? Do you want to work at some amazing company you've been looking at for years? No matter what it is, write it down as your main goal.

Is It About Getting a Bigger Paycheck?

There is nothing wrong about having a goal that involves money. You need money to live, to pay the bills, to provide food and education for children, for hobbies, for traveling, and more. Money can't buy happiness, but as long as you like what you do, making more of it can't hurt.

My advice is never quit your job to take a job you don't like just because it pays more. Many people don't like what they're doing for a living, but they keep the job because it pays well. Money is not the solution to everything. On the other hand, getting a bigger paycheck is as clear a goal as you can get: your goal is to make more money. But what can you do to get a bigger paycheck? Where should you apply? Do you need to get more experience? Change roles? Go back to school? Remember that your goal needs to be achievable (more on that later), so try to make it reasonable and write it down.

Is It About Getting More Visibility?

There are many reasons to want more visibility. You may want to grow your network. You may want to expand your pool of choice for your next job (in today's world, people often leave for a new challenge after five years at the same company). In any case, visibility can help you and is a valid goal. Visibility may be the goal, or it may be the path to reach your goal. Maybe you need more visibility because the new job you want needs it. That was my case when I targeted being an evangelist as my next step. If visibility is your goal or is required by your goal, write it down and continue to the next section.

Is It About Building New Skills or Competencies?

There are so many programming languages—maybe too many. It's a problem for me. I have had many languages on my to-learn list for years, but I can't even get my hands on new libraries for HTML, CSS, and JavaScript, which have been my primary focus for years. Skill and competency related to your job (or the job you want to get) can be a valuable goal.

Do you want to change your expertise and use another programming language for creating software? Maybe you want to gain more leadership skills and start managing people. Acquiring new skills or competencies is a goal that you can achieve in your present job. Employers are always looking for people who want to improve themselves and get better at their job. So write down your goal about learning something new or acquiring new competencies. (Or not. Maybe you're stagnated and don't want to learn anything more in your current job.)

Is It Some Other Goal?

The goals covered so far are the most common goals people have when it comes to their career, but seriously, a goal can be anything. As you've already seen in this book, I can write stuff down for days, but that's not the idea here. In the end, it's your personal brand, so you can achieve whatever you want with it. I focus a lot on the goal aspect of the brand, but maybe your goal is just to develop and manage your brand, be the owner of it, and make sure you control the message. It's easier to manage your brand if you have an ultimate goal. On the other hand, you may be totally happy where you are and with what you do—but you need to control your brand so others won't do it for you. If that's the case, I highly suggest you think about a more precise goal, because like I always say, there is always something you can improve on.

Your goal doesn't need to be only one specific thing. It can be a combination of several aspects. For example, you may want to change to a new position, and the new job pays the same as what you make now, but it's what you want to be doing. In that case, you may want to start with one goal (a job you like), and once you achieve it, go for the next one (a bigger paycheck). Later on, I talk about managing goals that are more complex, seem too big, or combine more than one aspect.

The Next Step Doesn't Have to Be Management

Too often, developers think that the next level must be about being a manager. It does not have to be. Managing may be one of your goals, and there's nothing wrong with it, but don't see that as the only path for you. If you like to create software, you can go from junior to senior to principal. You can find a new and exciting project, work in new companies, or find a different role that fits better with your life, like being a technical fellow (the most senior rank for a technical role in companies). There are plenty of opportunities for developers who want to continue to get things done.

Right now I have no intention of being a manager. I like being a technical evangelist. I went from junior to senior, and my next goal is to be a principal technical evangelist. Maybe my goal will change in the future, but for now, I still want to make things happen, work with developers, do presentations, and share my passion about technology. Again, I have nothing against managers or developers who go from creating software to managing a team—my point here is that it's not the only path.

Stairway to Heaven

I want to clarify something. Your goal should be as large as it has to be: think big. The sky's the limit. No, wait, the sky's not the limit—don't restrict yourself! Nothing is unattainable. The only thing you need to keep in mind to reach your personal career heaven is that it's easier if you use the stairs—if you go step by step. No matter how big your goal is, you need to think in terms of milestones to reach it.

Let's think of an example. How about being the lead developer of the well-known Web browser at a large technical company. That's an ambitious goal, and it's still feasible. Split that goal into interim steps, or milestones:

1. Get a developer job at the company.
2. Move to the browser team.
3. Become a senior developer in this team.
4. Become the lead developer of the browser.

The end goal is still the same; you want to become the lead developer on a specific team at the big company, but it's now broken down into four measurable steps. It's more concrete this way, and it feels more feasible than targeting the end goal right from the beginning without a plan. I'm pretty sure it's easier to enter the company first, in any role, than it would be to directly target the team's lead position.

Breaking a goal down into action steps can help you boost your morale and make it easier to create a plan on achieving your larger goal. It's like this with any task you want to do: if it's too big, create smaller steps to get there. Sometimes you can combine more than one step. For example, my previous goal was to go from developer to international senior technical evangelist. The idea behind it was about extending my network, visibility, and credibility. My first step was when I went from freelancer to technical evangelist at Microsoft. My territory was Canada. That was already a huge step, because I was getting visibility outside my city, Montréal. When I joined Mozilla, I turned two steps into one by landing a senior international role: I'm now traveling and speaking all over the world. In that case, I managed to combine two steps at once and can now move forward with the next step toward my goal.

Make It Quantifiable

Let's take one of the clearest examples: the goal of getting a better paycheck. Fine, you want more money, but how much more? It will be easier to know whether you succeed if you know exactly how much more money you want. Make your goals quantifiable. You need to be able to evaluate and measure them. You created a target, but how will you know if you hit the center or completely missed it? How will you know in 3, 6, or 12 months how you're doing, whether you're on target? It's nice to have a goal, but if there's no way for you to see your progress, reaching it will be hard.

You probably set goals in your performance evaluations. Do you define your goals for the year or a quarter as something vague, like "acquire more customers" or "give a better experience to our users"? No. Your manager wouldn't accept those goals because there's no way for him or her to know whether you did a great job of meeting them. What does *acquire more customers* mean? One? Five hundred? A million? It's the same thing for your goal: the more precise you are, the easier it will be to go from that goal to reality.

Setting Your Timeline: You Don't Have a TARDIS

Unless you're Doctor Who, you don't have access to a TARDIS. Meaning, you can't travel back in time to help your old self achieve your goal faster. This is also why you should be sure you are making progress along the way. Now that you know your goal should be quantifiable, you need to define a timeline. When will you achieve it? When should each of those steps be accomplished?

I don't know about you, but I'm *way* better when I have a deadline. A deadline helps prevent you from working on a never-ending goal or constantly pushing it to the back burner because it's not due yet. Even if you extend the timeline at some point because it wasn't realistic or because something happened beyond your control, you will still have a deadline. You would never tell your boss that the project you're working on will be finished "someday." He will want a much more precise idea of when it will be done.

Back to the example of being the team lead of the web browser at a big company, the following could be your timeline:

1. Get a developer job at the company: within 12 months.
2. Move to the browser team: 6 months after joining the company.
3. Become a senior developer in this team: 24 months after joining the company.
4. Become the lead developer of the browser: 42 months after joining the team.

If you look closer, the timeline turns out to be a five-year goal. Let's be honest, it's not an easy task being lead on that team—this company is huge, with a lot of brilliant people. You wouldn't be the only one targeting this job or this team. But let's be optimistic and still target a maximum of five years to achieve that goal. As I mentioned, you may skip some steps by combining them if that makes sense. You might get a job directly on the team as a developer if there is an opening role in that department when applying at the company. Maybe you're already part of the paid staff at that company, so this might be a three-step plan instead of four. Do you have more experience than the persona I had in mind while building this example? If yes, you may already get a senior role inside the company when they hire you. In any case, by splitting this goal up, it will be easier for you to reach it, no matter whether all the steps apply separately or not.

Note that I used months as the metric: it's a personal choice, but I prefer to use months instead of years, even for longer goals. It's mostly psychological. We all agree that 12 months equal one year, but somehow, calling it 12 months makes it easier to split your goal into smaller chunks. With one goal at a one-year stretch, it's easy to forget about it: *it's okay, the deadline is still far away.* Twelve months makes it more concrete: it's easier to see that you did nothing the last month if you have a monthly deadline. For smaller goals, you may use smaller metrics, like weeks or even days. This is a trick I use for everything that needs a deadline.

I would try to never have a subgoal (a smaller chunk) that takes longer than one year. I tend to lose track or leave too much for the last minute. So how about splitting those already-split tasks into more goals? Think about what you can do to reach those interim goals. An example of this may look like the following:

1. **Gather information about working at the company and how to handle the interview process: within 3 months.**
2. Get a developer job at the company: within the 12 months from the beginning of the overall goal.
3. Move to the browser team: 6 months after joining the company.
4. **Talk to three managers (two inside the browser team, and one in another department) about their vision of a senior developer role: 3 months after joining the browser team.**
5. **Update your goal and get the missing skills and competencies for the role: 6 months after talking to the managers.**
6. Become a senior developer on the team: 24 months after joining the company (9 months after working on your skills).
7. Become the lead developer of the browse: 42 months after joining the team.

Take a closer look at this new goal timeline: the modifications are in bold. Your end goal is the same: being the lead of the team within five years. You still have the goal to be a senior two years after joining the company, but new interim goals are there now. It usually takes about two years to move from junior to senior if you are doing a great job: it may take longer, but I rarely see people reaching that level without at least two years of experience. Because it's easy to forget that in two years you want to get a promotion, adding two steps to help you reach it is the key. Take the time to talk to some managers to get their ideas on the topic, let them form an opinion about you, and find out how they see the role of a senior developer. It's what I did when I was at Microsoft, but I left before being promoted. My experience and new skills were useful when I interviewed for Mozilla. Instead of saying you will take that time to acquire the missing skills or competencies, go ahead and define them as subgoals. Getting a job in a new company is not just about your skills or experience, so get more information on the culture, see how the interviews goes, and connect with actual employees. In the end, it's the same goal, but with this third iteration, you now have smaller steps. They should make it even easier to track your progress and realign yourself to get the most out of your effort and land your dream job.

Your Goal May Change, It Will Change, It Should Change

Like your brand, your goal will evolve with time. It can be about the goal itself: your interest may change, or you may find it's not for you anymore. It can be about the milestones: as mentioned, you may combine some steps, or may feel you still need to dig a bit deeper and split the steps you had previously in smaller ones. The timeline can change, too. You thought you would be able to get this new role within one year, but you got an offer three months after starting to focus on your dream job. What is the next step now? Or it may not be as easy as you thought, and it takes longer. No worries, it happens, and you don't have to be ashamed of it. Change your timeline when the step you're targeting is bigger than you thought or something unexpected gets in the way. Splitting goals into more reachable ones and adjusting the timeframe will help keep track of your progress.

It's not just about now: what happens when you reach your goal? Is there anything else? A new goal? Of course there is! There is always a next step. There is always something you can do next, something you can improve in your current situation. Even the best developers have something else they can achieve.

Goal setting, including the milestones and timeline, are what I did when I wanted to go from developer to evangelist. Now it's your turn to define your end goal (don't use a permanent pen—you can change it as often as you want):

I want to _____ **in** _____ **months.**

Keep in mind that this is your *ultimate* goal now, but it will change. If it feels too big or unreachable, split it into many subgoals and add the necessary timeframe to them. Together, they will be the steps you need to take to achieve what you just wrote in those lines.

So you've got the basic stuff done: defining your goal. It will be easier to focus on your brand once you know what you want to achieve and why you're working on your personal branding. It will help you prioritize actions and learn how to say no—but that's a topic we'll talk about later.

How Can You Differentiate Yourself?

Before going deeper into defining your brand, let's review an important concept: you need to differentiate yourself from others. I'm not talking about your unique skills. I don't think there are any unique skills in our industry: there is usually someone, somewhere, who has the same competencies as you, even if yours is in a niche. On the other hand, you may not have the same level of expertise: you may be better than this other person, or have a niche inside a niche. You can be the best Python developer out there; there are many other Python developers. Can it still be something that differentiates you from others? Of course! It can also be a specialty that not a lot of people have. Maybe you're an amazing Scala developer as well. It can be a combination of many aspects of your brand that can help you differentiate from the crowd. Maybe you're the best PHP developer using PostgreSQL on Windows. It can also be about location: you may be the best JavaScript developer in your area. The key is to think differently.

Why is differentiation so important? It's simple: if we all had the same branding, how would you be able to get out of the crowd? How would you stand out from others and get the visibility you need? We're all different—and you need to *highlight* that difference. Once in a while, I lecture in schools about working in IT. One of the main points of these presentations is how students can differentiate themselves—in other words, personal branding. In the end, all the students in the class had the same courses, did the same homework, will get the same diploma, and will finish school at the same time. Sure, there are some differences in how they did their homework and took their tests. But they need to differentiate themselves if they want to get the job or the internship they want: they are all competing against each other!

When I worked at a startup, we were three developers doing mostly web development with nearly the same experience in the technology we were using. How was I able to differentiate myself from others? I was the guy doing mobile development on the team, and I was good at QA (quality assurance). So even if I had mostly the same skills as my teammates, I was able to differentiate myself. Now, as a technical evangelist, I can focus on some aspect of it that my colleagues don't have. At the same time, they can differentiate themselves from me with other expertise or experience. It's a matter of finding what makes you unique.

Don't Be a Copy Cat, But . . .

Remember Chapter 1's examples of people with strong brands? Remember that quick exercise I asked you to do in which you listed some people with a strong brand? I want you to do that again, but this time focus strictly on two or three people who have a personal brand you like, a brand you would like to have. Feel free to use the same people you used earlier if it makes sense.

What do these people have in common? Is it the fact that they speak at conferences? Is it about the visibility they get in the field? Maybe it's the fact that they seem amazing when they blog about Ruby tips and tricks. What do you like about their brand? No matter who they are, where they live, whether they are international superstars or the developers at the shop in your small town, they are models. Think about them and list what they have in common that you like. You'll be able to use this as the big picture for what could be your brand. It's not about copying their style, getting the same expertise they have, or trying to emulate what they did or are doing. It's just to give you an idea, a canvas to work with. You don't have to base your brand on these examples, but it may help you define what you want your brand to be, and it will certainly be a good starting point.

What Is Your Actual Brand?

There was an exercise in Chapter 3 in which you asked some people to define you. I suggested it was important and that we would use it in a future chapter. I hope they didn't just focus on your personal aspects, but on everything that defines you: your job, your expertise, your sense of humor, and so on. A big part of personal branding is about how people see you. I bet you were a bit anxious when I wrote that you had to *build* your personal brand: after all, you're not going to create fiction. Your brand will be made of two parts of yourself:

1. Who you are
2. Who you want to be

Be careful here, it's not about *inventing* something. I want to be sure you understand that fact, because it's important. If you build your brand on something false, it will hit you back, and you won't like it. You brand should be roughly 80% who you are, and 20% what you want to surface, change, be better at, or be recognized for. We'll come back on the last 20% later. For now, let's focus on the bigger and more important part: who you are right now.

Chapter 3 focused on the personal side of your brand or, shall we say, *yourself*. We focused on everything that defines you as a person, without thinking about the career side. You'll use that part here. We'll add everything else that defines you, mostly professional aspects. At first, this may feel a bit weird: as if you don't know who you are or what makes you as awesome as you are. Still, it's a good thing to define those points, even if it's to confirm what you already know. You would also be surprised to know how many people *don't* know themselves. It's okay if you're one of them; the next section is all for you.

The Trilogy of Your Life: Past, Present, and Future

The professional side of your brand is based on the present, on who you are right now—but also on the past, as well as the future. As we work on the first 80% (who you are), let's start with the past, because that's what helped you become who you are and be where you are right now.

What do you want to highlight from your past experience? What achievement stands out in your résumé? What are you proudest of? Which companies did you work for? Do you want to highlight an international project you participated at your previous company? Do you want to talk about the prizes your team won in an internal competition? Is it about how you manage your team to achieve a huge rate of success for your customers? Maybe it's the company you built and the fact that you have employees now? No matter what, highlight everything that makes sense—we will use it all later.

"But Fred, I'm a student. I don't have work experience. Are you telling me I can't build my brand?" Of course not. No worries, there are many things you can add. What about some cool projects you did for a specific class? Did you have an internship where you led an innovative, creative project the company did not have the time to build previously? Were you contributing to some open-source projects? What about jobs you had as a student, even if they weren't related to IT?

No matter if you're a seasoned developer or haven't even started to work in a company, there are many items you can add to your list. Think about what you did when you created your first résumé: even without any experience, you were able to fill a page, weren't you? The idea is to put in things that will create a wow effect—anything you're proud of or anything you find useful. No need to be the winner of five Pulitzer Prizes to have a personal brand!

As an example, when I did this exercise when updating my own brand and looking for a new job, I highlighted some facts of my career (in no particular order):

- Expertise with web (HTML5) and different mobile technologies
- Career path toward startup, small company, freelance, and Fortune 500
- More than 10 years in the IT industry, with nearly 3 years as a technical evangelist
- Led the Canadian open-source initiative Make Web Not War, and outreach at Microsoft
- Founded HTML5mtl (450 members at that time), Failcamp Montréal (full house on the first edition), and Festival Geek de Montréal (750+ attendees in the second year)

This list is facts, not fluff. It does not mean those are the only things I'm proud of or can highlight. Think about it as a summary of your résumé by highlighting the best points. In fact, the more stuff you have, the harder it will be to have a consistent brand. In my example, the reasons for including those particular things were mostly to showcase my varied experience and that I'm a doer: I make stuff. I emphasized my expertise with web and mobile technologies because I was looking for a technical evangelist role focusing on the web and/or mobility. They were two of my interests in technology. I had a chance to work in a small company (my first job) and in a startup; I started my own company as a freelancer and worked for one of the biggest companies out there, Microsoft. All of this shows I can adapt to different types of enterprises and situations. There's nothing wrong if you don't have experience yet. We were all newbies at one point. But since I was in the industry for more than 10 years, I wanted to let people know I had experience. Not just as a developer, but because I was looking for an evangelist job, that this kind of job was not a new concept for me. Because I was one of the leaders of the Make Web Not War initiative (http://webnotwar.ca), I wanted to showcase that open source was my job, even if I was at Microsoft (which is not considered one of the most fervent open-source companies). By leading this initiative and focusing on events and the user group I created (with the help of amazing people), the highlight of my past was that I'm a doer. I can take an idea and make it a reality.

It may sound like bragging, but it's like passing an interview: you need to showcase what you've done, and it's the same with your brand. If you haven't yet done it, take the time to list some high points of the last few years of your career. You'll use those to build your personal brand and refine your elevator pitch.

Living the Moment

The past clearly shaped who you are right now, but is there anything else you want to add? Is there a programming language you would like to master, or something else that can be part of your brand? To help jog your brain, I'll give you a couple of questions to answer. Take your time. Answer the ones that make sense for you. Feel free to add anything you think I missed. Write them down on paper or in a digital document. You'll use those answers to finally come up with a proper personal brand.

1. What is the programming language you're primarily using or know best?
2. Are you a Linux, Windows, or OS X user?
3. Is your expertise about mobile application, web development, a standalone one, or a mix of those answers?
4. To git or not to git?
5. Do you have an amazing knowledge about TDD (test-driven development) and can't imagine that developers don't test their applications before releasing them?
6. Is open source your friend or enemy?
7. Do you have any certifications?
8. Is the command line the only way to go?
9. iOS, Android, Windows Phone, Firefox OS, BlackBerry? Which mobile platform is your best friend?
10. Have you been recognize by an industry leader as a contributor (like a Mozilla Rep or MVP [Microsoft Most Valuable Professional])?
11. Are you already running a technical blog?
12. Are you an advocate of Mobile First or Responsive Web Design?
13. Where are you working right now?
14. Do you contribute to technical online magazines?
15. Do you help or assist often with local user groups?
16. Is it true that HTML5 has no secrets for you?
17. Are you part of a local IT organization?

18. Do you prefer books, audiobooks, podcasts, e-books, online articles, blog posts, and so on to learn when it comes to technology?
19. Are you a team player, or better as a lone wolf?
20. Waterfall or Sprint? Maybe you are a Scrum Master?
21. Google+, Twitter, Facebook, LinkedIn . . . which is your preferred social media platform?
22. Are you part of a bigger mission than you, like the Open Web?
23. Do you work on projects in your spare time?
24. Are you a fervent user of Vim, Sublime Text, Eclipse, Visual Studio, or Xcode?
25. Which side are you: native or web mobile application?
26. What is your actual job title?
27. Do you already run a monthly podcast about application development?
28. Do you consider yourself a geek?

Those answers, or at least the ones that make sense for you, will help you further in this chapter. Trust me, you have not done this in vain.

The Last 20%: Be a Seer

Now let's focus on what you can change and improve, and where you want to go: the last 20%. I repeat: this is not about lying, but it's also not limited to who you are right now, either. Let me explain.

In life, there is always room for improvement . Are there any skills you would like to improve? Maybe you need a competency for a new job, or there's something you already know or have but would like to take to the next level. Maybe you use git now, but would like to refine your skills by using GitHub (or any other online repository) a bit more to achieve a more impressive contribution summary on your profile. Is there a skill you already have that people don't know at all, or that you would like to make more visible?

In my case, I wanted to get better at public speaking and get more speaking gigs. It's why *public speaker* is part of my brand. (Actually, I added *international public speaker* right after I first spoke in the United States. At that time, I had only spoken in two countries, but still, it was true: I *was* an international public speaker.) Because my goal was to speak in more countries, I wanted to highlight this. Remember my example about doing some iOS development, how people were referring to me as an iOS developer when I was a freelancer? At that time, my website was offering this platform, and I added it in my Twitter bio. But as you may also remember, I had no experience in it. It was part of my 20%, the aspect of my brand I wanted to change.

Unleashing the Kraken

I don't want you to destroy everything and everyone around you, but you need to release the beast. It's what you've been waiting for: you will put everything you've listed into a melting pot to create your brand:

1. Who you are on a personal level (remember the questions you answered in Chapter 3)
2. What you've done on a professional level
3. Who you are, right now, on a professional level
4. What differentiates you from others
5. Who you want to be or what you can improve (look into the future)

Think about all aspects of your personal and professional life. Don't forget what you put in your elevator pitch, because it may still be relevant. Think about the elevator pitch as a subset of your brand. You can always come back later to finish, but I encourage you to take the time to do this exercise, because it will be your brand, this one snapshot in time. I suggest you define your brand in a couple of sentences, but with enough details (more than in the pitch) so it will be totally clear for you. Remember those biographies you read in the conference schedule? It should not be longer than those. Check over everything you have written. Leave in only the things that will have a real impact and represent you better.

As an example, let's see the last version of my own brand: a longer, more complete version of the elevator pitch.

> *I am a developer who has used many programming languages, but who is now focusing on web technology like HTML, CSS, and JavaScript. I've worked in different types of company: small ones, Fortune 500 ones like Microsoft, and startups, and have even been a freelancer. I've worked on mobile and web applications that were either very local, used by hundreds of people, or were competing (and winning) against worldwide enterprises. I'm an open source guy with a pragmatic view on things. I'm now a senior technical evangelist at Mozilla and I like to share my passion and technical expertise with the rest of the world, mostly about the web and Firefox OS. In the past three years I've given more than 100 talks in 13 countries. I love the web, music, and people. I'm a longtime blogger and*

a social beast. I'm transparent, talk too much, and always wear cool geek T-shirts. If I don't like something, I don't do it. If I don't enjoy something, I move on to the next thing. My goal in life is to be completely happy. I'm also a serial entrepreneur, what you would call a doer: I like to take an idea and make a project out of it. Once it's successful, I move on to something else. I stay true to myself, always. I always wear jeans and a T-shirt, even when everybody else is dressed up: it's part of my brand, how people identify me. I'm bored easily, and a procrastination expert. I also want to improve myself and be more efficient in my life, not just on the professional side. I want to continue to be better as an evangelist and continue to share my love of technologies. I want to reach the next level as a principal evangelist.

It's not too long: enough details for me to stay focused on my brand. I included all elements of the five points: who I am on a personal level, what I've done as a professional, who I am right now professionally, what differentiates me from others, and who I want to be. You need to write the truth. I admit that I'm an expert at procrastinating. I know myself, and I can make things work and achieve things even if it's at the last minute. I may have to force myself to set a deadline even when others don't need one. Okay, time for you to get to it and write your brand!

Let's try redefining your elevator pitch as a tweet to see if it has changed. You always need to have both versions up to date—the longer one will be your guide to help you attend your goal, and the shorter one (elevator pitch) will be what you use to sell yourself to the rest of the world. There is no need to lose yourself in a full paragraph when you talk to others. You should be able to state it in a sentence, as before, but with the full picture. A lot more details (the longer brand statement you wrote) will help you drive your actions. Your elevator pitch can help you focus to make something complex into something simple. Remember, with a tweet you only have 140 characters to define your elevator pitch. As Mr. Miyagi said to Daniel in *The Karate Kid*, *focus*. It's not permanent—you can update it as often as you want.

I'm curious to see if your tweet changed after the last couple of chapters. Were you right on the spot? Did it change completely? This is what you will focus on for the rest of the book. This is your brand, the brand you already had without being conscious of it. It's a brand that will drive your actions every day of your life. This is . . . you!

Half the Work Is Done

You are now more conscious about your personal brand because you have defined it. Who you are and how you want people to see you are now written down. Remember, it's not set in stone, at least for now—everything can and should change. It's only the first part of the story: you still have to take control of your image and lead your brand. The following chapters show how you can achieve this and shine with all the awesomeness that is your personal brand.

CHAPTER

5

Do Epic Stuff
The How

Do or do not. There is no try.

—Yoda

Let's start this chapter by introduced a developer I know: David Walsh who is a great coder. David writes a technical blog (http://davidwalsh.name), which is quite popular. He's not a technical evangelist, but a developer, like you, doing an amazing job with his personal brand. I asked him the same questions that appear in previous chapters.

In answer to my question "Do you think personal branding is important for a developer, and why?" David was unambiguous. He firmly believes that personal branding is important:

> *Absolutely. Developers deserve credit for their hard work, especially when they provide their code or knowledge to the general community free of charge. Personal branding is also a massive help in advancing a developer's career. You put a name to a body of work.*

It's clear that David's brand helped him get his dream job, but it also helped him on the personal side:

> I owe where I am today, both personally and professionally, to personal branding with my blog. My blog, named after myself, has allowed me to move from a small print shop in Madison, Wisconsin, to Mozilla, a dream career move. Obviously a pay and benefits bump came with that move, and as a result I've been able to move into a nicer home, start a family, and take vacations to places we've dreamed of going. I've been able to fly around the world and speak at events, as well as meet great people and work on exciting projects. I owe much of my happiness to the rewards that personal branding brought me.

Last but not least, David has some advice for you:

> Creating a blog with personal branding is the best way to showcase your knowledge and talent. Getting involved in open-source initiatives that you're passionate about will also open doors for your career. GitHub has become the new résumé, so ensure you make your account visible. Last, give yourself credit in all of your work—you deserve it.

David's advice fits well with this chapter (Chapter 6 goes into more detail on everything he shared with you here). I cover blogging and contributing to an open-source project by using services like GitHub.

The How

Are you excited? I hope so. You defined your personal brand in Chapter 4 by consolidating everything you learned. Now it's time for action! Here, you'll see how you can go from the idea of having a personal brand to managing it and making it happen. It's one thing to be conscious that you have a personal brand; it's another to actually use it and take it to the next level to reach your goals. I list some ways you can make your personal brand come alive. In combination with the next chapters, you'll learn the secret weapons that can help you achieve the how. As developers, we are lucky—there are many ways to help us in the journey. It's one advantage of loving the technology: it gives us the power to access many tools. Remember, now is almost too late, so let's not lose any more time. Let's learn more about achieving your personal brand.

Be Naive

There is a saying that stupid people are happier, probably because they don't overthink situations. In a sense, I want you to be stupid. Maybe you think you don't have time to manage your brand on top of everything else you have to do, like your job, raising a family, going to the gym, and cleaning the house. Again, be "stupid"! Leave those fears alone. Don't feed them. You'll find that it's easier than you think. This chapter will help you see how you can integrate the management of your personal brand into your day-to-day job and the rest of your life.

There Is No Try

I'm a huge fan of *Star Wars*. I don't want to start a fight here, but everybody knows it's better than *Star Trek*. (I may as well have written, "Please, *Star Trek* fans, throw my book in the garbage!") All joking aside, I like Yoda's wisdom, and his quote at the beginning of this chapter resonates with me: "Do or do not. There is no try."

You are at the crossroads of this book. It's time to not *try* working on your personal brand but actually *do* it. When you tell yourself that you'll try, you set yourself up for failure. You give yourself an excuse not to succeed. After all, you didn't say you would do it, but that you would try to do it. I'm a proud person, so whenever I set goals for myself, since I told myself I was going to do it, I usually push to make it happen because I don't want to admit I did not accomplish it. If you are like this too, you can commit to your friends, family, colleagues, or even online: commit yourself publicly to working on your brand or toward your ultimate goal. It will motivate you.

It's a Question of Passion

I'm pretty sure you would not be so good with your preferred programming language if you were not passionate about technology and about the language. We will explore together different ways to achieve your goals with your brand, but if you are not passionate about your brand and what you'll do to achieve it, I'm afraid you will fail. As much as I like learning from my failures, if I can avoid failing, I prefer to take that path.

Don't Plan Like an Underpants Gnome

An episode of *South Park* caught my attention because it featured underpants gnomes. They have a goal in life: to make profit. We don't know the reason, but they want to make money. To achieve their goal, they have a plan:

1. Collect underpants.
2. ?
3. Profit!

Do you think their plan is missing something? They know what to do and what they want as their end goal, but they don't know how they will reach that goal from their actions. I use this example in some of my presentations because I think it's funny. Many people have goals and hope they will reach them "one day." But they have no plan to help them get there.

Nothing happens by magic. That's what this chapter is about. You start with an idea, you take action, and the profit will be the realization of the goals you defined in the previous chapter. Don't be an underpants gnome—you won't make profits just because you wish to.

Impact and Scale

During my time at Microsoft, I had the pleasure of working with Ryan Storgaard. He gave me a lot of good advice and helped me become the technical evangelist I am today. One piece of wisdom he shared with me was about the impact and scalability of my work. It was true for a role like mine, and it might be even truer with something like personal branding. Every time you do something related to your brand, you think about those important words: impact and scale. Can I have more impact? Is there a way to scale to the next level my actions?

Impact

Thinking about the impact of what you do will help you decide what you want to do and what is most important. Thinking about impact is a tool to help you prioritize. Go with what makes the biggest impact and makes the most sense for you. It will always depend on your goal.

Let's say you have one hour before bedtime. You want to do something that will help your brand. Of course, watching television won't help you at all. So what could you do? Let's say your short-term goal is to start speaking in public. You might write a status update on Facebook mentioning the fact that you are open to speaking gigs. It will help you share the message across your network of friends and people who know you. Instead, why not put in a little more effort and make it into a blog post discussing the reasons developers should speak? You could add a note inside the post about the fact that you are looking for speaking opportunities. By taking this slightly different approach, you become useful to others instead of just promoting yourself. You also have a better chance of snaring people's interest. By putting this on your blog, you make your content more accessible to search engines, and you make it more likely that a stranger will find your post. Of course, you can promote your post on Facebook afterward. Your blog post will have a longer life span, as the longevity of posts on social media websites are not very long. Maybe you can find something else even more useful, with a bigger impact—you get the point. Even if it takes more than an hour, or a few nights, the impact makes it worth it.

My friend Julien Smith co-wrote a book with Chris Brogan on the topic: *The Impact Equation: Are You Making Things Happen or Just Making Noise?* (Portfolio, 2012). This book talks about every aspect of having a real impact, including the authors' warning that you can think you are having an impact, but in reality you might just be making noise.

Scale

Scale is important. No matter what you do, if it does not scale, you won't be successful. Personal branding is not necessarily a game of numbers, but if your brand doesn't reach anyone, and what you do and believe in does not affect anyone, it won't do you any good. Of course, you need to think about scaling in combination with impact.

As a public speaker, when I go on stage at a conference, I reach a certain number of people. Let's say there are 200 people in the room. Do you agree that in the end, the topic I was talking about has reached 200 people? Probably not everyone was listening, but let's pretend it was the perfect crowd (between you and me, the perfect crowd does not exist—there are always people who don't listen no matter how interesting you are). If I did a great job, those developers may talk to their friends or colleagues about the technology I showed them. So I may gain more visibility than just the people in the room, but my reach is still low for the effort I put in preparing my outline, learning the content (if it was something new), building the slides, and the one hour or so I was in front of the crowd. What can I do to help scale my talk a bit more without too much effort?

First, I will publish my slides online. The slides without the talk itself don't have that much impact, since they are only visual aids, but I will reach a couple more hundred people than I may have otherwise. Even if they don't understand all of my presentation, they will know I understand this topic by seeing my slides online—or at least, they will know they can talk to me or ask me questions about it.

I also record my talk and upload it to YouTube. Some conferences provide recording services. Most of the time, I do it myself. Through YouTube, not only will I reach another few hundred people, I will be able to share the exact vision I had with this talk, which will be way better than the slides alone. I do a combination of publishing my slides and videos on sites where it makes sense to do so.

Once those two things are done, I write a blog post about my experience at the conference or give some highlights from the talk. I also point to the slides and embed video into the post. That will add my readers to the crowd I reach with my presentation and help Google remember me and my talk.

Last but not least, I promote the post I just wrote on different social media websites like Twitter, Facebook, LinkedIn, and Google+. By using the official hashtag of the event (if there is one) I'll be able to scale to another level. Quite often, many people who were unable to attend the conference will follow it on Twitter.

By doing all that, using the power of modern media, I scaled quite a bit. I went from reaching 200 people to a *lot* more. This is one example of how you can take something you have done and scale it up. Of course, all that took some effort, but the result is impressive. I'll come back to using technological tools in the next chapter.

Don't forget to use your network, as I did with my blog post about my talk. The people you know and the people who know you can help you scale. Chapter 7 is entirely about your tribe: that gives you an idea of how important and critical social media is when it comes to personal branding and, of course, achieving your goals.

Do Stuff. No, Do Epic Stuff!

I told you that doing epic shit is my mantra—not just for personal branding but everything in life. If you remember one thing from this chapter, it's this: do stuff. Do stuff that matters. Don't be a talker. Make thing happen. It's the most important secret I can tell you. By doing things, you will achieve your goal. There are plenty of things you can do, and that's what this chapter is all about.

By *epic*, I mean big and bold. Of course, small actions can help you realize your goals—but you can do bigger things, too. Would you benefit from a user group about Objective-C (or Swift, the new programming language from Apple)? What, there's no group in your area? You'll have to find someone who would like to start the group. Why not start it yourself? Think big about your goals, and think big about the actions you'll take to make your brand a reality.

Let's see some concrete examples (in no particular order) of what you can do to help your brand:

- Start a blog.
- Be a proctor at a hackathon.
- Write guest blog posts.
- Start an audio podcast.

- Create a conference or other industry event.
- Start a video podcast.
- Write open-source code.
- Find a mentor.
- Write for magazines (online or print).
- Organize an unconference or a camp-style event.
- Grow your network.
- Write a book.
- Be a mentor at a workshop.
- Create applications or games.
- Volunteer.
- Do public speaking.
- Contribute to an open-source project.
- Start a user group.
- Use social media.
- Mentor someone with less experience than you.
- Go to (and participate in) networking events.

The list could go on for quite a while, and your imagination is the only limit. Because this chapter is more on the form of things, on the high level of the "how," we'll go elaborate later on why those actions may be beneficial and how you can do them. Take the time to read the rest of this chapter and the next to learn what tools you can use to make your brand amazing.

Nobody likes people who talk but take no action. Don't do it only for the trophies. I know too many people who have taken a position on a board of directors but do nothing. That's taking credit when it isn't deserved. On the outside, you look like a doer, someone who helps the industry, helps others, and is making things happen. But you're not fulfilling your role and don't really deserve whatever comes with what you were supposed to do.

Learn to Say No

Saying no is something I'm getting better at. I have trouble saying no. Sometimes it's hard for me to say no to others—and even to myself. I like to help others, and I always have millions of ideas I would like to make happen. We only have a finite number of days to live, and there are only 24 hours in a day.

That means that we need to prioritize and choose what will have the most impact. I'm sure there are many things you would like to do to help your brand, but you can't do everything. I'm sure there are many people you can help, but you can't help them all. Choose your battles. Saying no is not easy for some people, but it's a crucial skill if you want to be successful.

As an example, I started the GeekFestMtl (Festival Geek de Montréal). It was an amazing experience to build a team and create this festival from scratch. It's something I'm proud of, and I know that my "core geek team" is proud, too. We managed to get more than 750 people to attend the second festival. Unfortunately, it was taking a lot of my time, and even though I liked it so much, I decided to let it go. It was not easy. Now I know how founders feel when their startups are acquired by another company (though at least they get money for it). It was time for me to use those couple of hours a week to relax a little bit, have more time with friends and family, and work on projects that would have a better impact or at least that would be more related to my end goal of being a technical evangelist.

The festival certainly helped my personal brand and made me known a little more in my city. I also made great contacts, including in the local media. It solidified my reputation as a doer, because it was something people were able to see, something concrete. I also gained experience that helped me do other things, like start a user group. I firmly believe that no experience is wasted. But as I said, I had to focus, and I said no to myself.

It's not just about you, remember. The more people know you, the more your brand will shine, and the more people will ask you for help. Don't deny every request. It's important to give some of your time, but you need to be able to focus. As an example, I got two book offers before this one, and another while I was writing this book. I said no to one because the editor did not want to use my chapter outline, and what they were proposing to me did not fit what I had in mind. Remember, you need to stay true to yourself, and if I were going to write a few hundred pages, they should at least make sense to me as the author. The offer I got while writing this book was on a topic I wanted to write about, but I felt I could only handle one book at a time. The first offer was on a topic outside my expertise. I had related expertise, and would have probably been able to write it, but it would have taken me more time than it should for an expert. Except for being able to use it to say that I'm a writer, I would have no direct benefit from accepting the offer. I had to say no. You think it put me on the editor's blacklist? Not at all! They were happy that I was honest with them. In fact, they are the ones who offered me three of the four book writing deals I got (the fourth one being for this book).

Success in Programming

I also read somewhere that "no" is a complete sentence. It does not need justification. So learn how to use this word—sorry, sentence—to yourself and to others. Focus on what makes sense for you, for your brand, and for your goal. To help you (and me), I created the graphic shown in Figure 5-1.

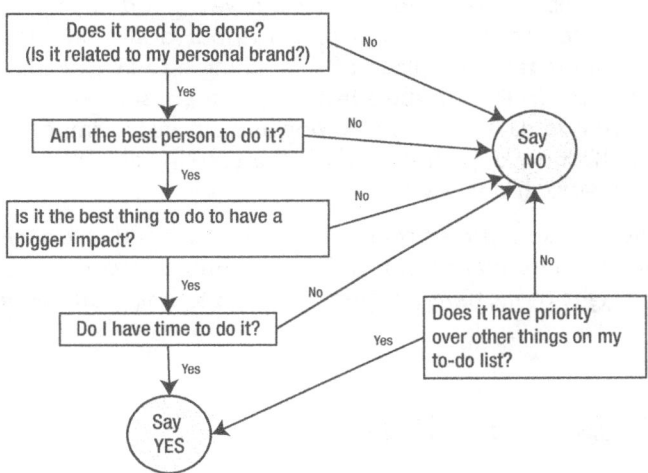

Figure 5-1. How to say no

Let me go into a little more detail on saying no, using Figure 5-1 as a starting point:

1. Does it need to be done, or in other words, is it related to your personal brand? If not, don't do it.

2. Are you the best person to do it? You need to prioritize, and even if something would make sense for your brand, maybe you are not the best person to do it. Maybe you don't have the expertise or it's not the right time. It may be something you need to do with the goal of adding the experience to your portfolio. In that case, go for it. In any situation, use your common sense.

3. If it needs to be done, and you are the right person to do it, how impactful is it? Remember, you need to prioritize some ideas and tasks to be sure you'll get the most return on investment with the effort you'll put in your branding.

4. Do you have time? Too often, people tend to say yes to a lot of amazing things and then figure out after the fact they don't have the time to do it and deliver a quality result. If you have the time to do it, go ahead, but if not, you need to ask yourself one last question.

5. If the job needs to be done, will have a good impact, and you are the best person to do it, but don't have time, should it take the place of something else at the top of your to-do list? Maybe something you considered imperative two days ago is still important, but not as important as this new opportunity. If it's the case, go ahead and do the work. If not, say no!

Keep in mind that sometimes there are things we need to do even if they're not part of our personal brand. Using my simple algorithm can help you focus on the right thing, have a bigger impact, and help you say no when you need to.

Don't Live in the Future

You don't have to wait to start working on your brand. There are plenty of things you can do right now, on your actual job, even if what you do now doesn't have a lot of relation to what you want to do next.

You will need to think about it, but there are many ways to include some of your action items in your job. You could start writing some blog posts to show your expertise on a particular topic. Is it a technology you use at work? If so, you should ask your manager if you can start a blog or write for the company one. It will be a way to work on your personal brand during working hours. Your blog would help the business, as you would prove to customers that you have good expertise. You could also create interest, find new employees, or increase exposure in the community. Of course, your name would be attached to those posts, and you will be able to add them to your portfolio.

Maybe you want to be a Scrum Master, but there is already one in your team. Why not take some courses now, even if there is no open position? If your manager is thinking long term, he may agree to sign you up for the courses. In the end, if another person has extensive knowledge about the Scrum framework, it will help the team. You could also ask your current Scrum Master for some advice. He will be able to teach you his skills and understand his role from his own perspective.

Think about what *you* can do right now. Almost any solution you find, and any way you decide to make things happen more quickly, will help you achieve your goal faster.

Make It Art and Go the Extra Mile

A good starting point is to be sure your work is a piece of *Art*, with a capital A, as Seth Godin says. I don't mean be pretentious here. I am a good developer, but not the best one out there. I am a great technical evangelist, but not the best in the world. But every time I do something, I try to make it worthwhile. Make it Art.

They say code is poetry. Make your code a poem, even if you don't like your job or the project. You should deliver something you're proud of. It's your reputation, and reputation is critical. If everybody agrees that I'm arrogant, unprofessional, unfriendly, or anything else negative, no matter where I am or what my brand is, I won't succeed. People won't work with me, won't refer customers to me, and won't give me a job, and that's not the result I want. Do a good job no matter what.

Your customer asked you to add a simple map into her application to let customers find her location easily. Why not create a custom icon on the map and provide an option to get directions from the user's location? You're a good developer—it won't take you much time, and the experience will be much better for the user. Your customer, who asked for a simple map, will be more than happy. I'm sure the next time she needs a new feature for her site or the software you built for her (or new applications or sites), she will think about you. She may refer you to others because you went the extra mile. I'm not saying you should go overboard and do a lot of work for free, but I'm sure you got the point.

One of my goals at work has been to help developers be successful. I thought we were doing a great job, but I wondered if we weren't missing an audience that could help us reach our goal. I proposed to work on a program to help us scale a bit more and reach new developers to my manager. The idea was to connect with different user groups all across the world and offer them support. Some of those groups have asked us to give more information about our technology to their users and will give us the opportunity to reach people we haven't talked to before. The program just started. I can't wait to see where it leads. This is an idea that benefits both me and my team.

Every Word You Say Will Be Used Against You

I'm not a police officer or a lawyer, but trust me, every word you say can and will be used against you. Does that mean you should stop talking? Not at all. (I would die if I had to shut up: I did a silent retreat for two days once, and it was definitely time to go back to reality!) People will remember what you said most of the time. Humans don't have perfect memories, but the Internet does. Whatever you write online—no matter if it's on Twitter, Facebook,

Google+, your blog, in a forum, or in the comments section of a website—never dies. The Internet knows and will remember. So you need to be careful. Think about what you say and what you put online, because it may have an impact in the future.

On the other hand, when I have an opinion about something, and when I want to share it, I just do it. Of course, there is a chance people will misinterpret what I meant, but most of the time people get what I had in mind. I learned that after Mozilla hired me, some people thought I was too direct in my approach. That was not a surprise. I know who I am, and I go right to the point, no matter what the subject is. That could have cost me my job, but I decided to stay true to myself, and you should, too. Even so, every word I had written online could have been used against me.

Out of Your Comfort Zone Is Where the Magic Happens

Is it scary to go outside of your comfort zone (see Figure 5-2)? It can be. Why would you want to do stuff that you are not comfortable with? Simply because that is often where growth happens and you'll see your efforts pay off. You have to go out of your comfort zone to achieve more, do more, have a bigger impact, and help your brand reach the next level.

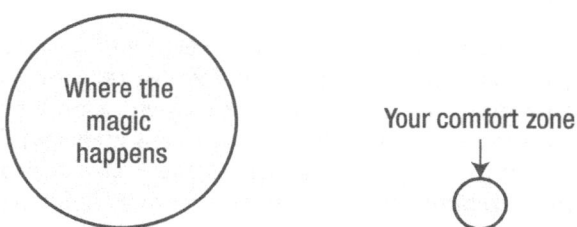

Figure 5-2. Out of your comfort zone is where the magic happens

Besides the pride that comes with doing something you're not used to, the more you do things that are outside of your comfort zone, the bigger your comfort zone gets. Have you had any issues writing documentation for your projects? Maybe you've been unsure about the syntax, what to include, whether it was totally useful, or just in general about your writing. After all, you're a coder, not a writer. But if you've done a lot of it, you've gotten better. Maybe you even enjoy it by now.

The beauty of getting used to going out of your comfort zone is that you can apply it to your everyday life, not just your personal branding. One rock, two hits. I highly suggest you read the free e-book from Julien Smith called *The Flinch* (The Domino Project, 2011). It will help you get out of your comfort zone, confront your fears, and change your mind-set.

The Easiest Path Is Not Shameful

I see no problem taking the easiest path if it's available to me. I don't understand people who avoid doing things that are "too easy." Why should I wait another two years to get that promotion if I can get it within one year? Of course, I'm not talking about lying or cheating to reach my goals.

I became a freelancer because I lost my job. I didn't have a lot of money saved up and didn't have time to prepare myself very well—it's not like I had planned to quit my job to start my own business. I found out about a program for entrepreneurs in my area and added my name on the list. The nonprofit organization (helped by the government) accepted my application, so I joined the program to help new entrepreneurs start their enterprises. The idea was simple: for a couple of weeks, we worked on our business plans, built our companies, and began acquiring customers as business deals. We had some courses on various topics to help us and also received mentoring. They were helping us financially, too. I was getting money, so I was able to put food on the table during the time I was building my future. It was a good program, but I left before the end when I got a job offer I could not refuse. During the year I was a freelancer, I got some customers, worked on different projects, and received the help of this association—which made things easier for me. Was my success less impressive than someone who was eating ramen and peanut butter toast while they got on their feet? I don't think so. We both worked hard to create something we were proud of, but I used a program that was available to me.

Don't Be Afraid to Ask

Maybe it goes hand in hand with taking the easiest path, but don't be afraid to ask for what you want. In the worst case, the other person will say no. By not asking, the result will be likely the same: as if the person said no. If you ask for what you want or need, there is a chance that the answer will be yes. Don't wait to see if that specific person will maybe one day think that you might want something and contact you about it. If they say no, at least you tried!

Part of my job involves public speaking, and I have many other tasks as well. I wanted to change the ratio of those tasks and do more public speaking, because it's something I enjoy a lot. (Plus, public speaking is way more important than people think—it's how we inspired developers to use the open web, and without that, I wouldn't be able to do the rest of my job.) I could have waited to see whether my manager would come up with the idea on his own. Maybe he has some superpower that gives him the ability to read my mind. (I doubt it.) So I told him about it. The worst-case scenario would have been him saying no. Instead, he agreed to it, and we set up a plan to be sure I'm talking more but not neglecting my other tasks. This is a happy ending story: I tried and succeeded. Maybe days, months, or years later he would have thought of it and offered me the change of duties I wanted, but I took the lead, asked him, and got the result right away.

FOMO

FOMO means *fear of missing out*. One thing that will happen as you read the next pages is a desire to do everything I'm about to write about. I need to warn you: there is no way you can do everything—at least, not at the beginning. If you try it, you may end up with low-quality work and of course low-quality results. I've been doing these things for years. Some of them are also part of my tasks at work, as my role involves personal branding. It's easy for me to do many of these tasks because I've had a lot of practice.

It's also easy to fear that you're going to miss something, so it's important to prioritize. There is no way you can assist at every event you would like to, for example. It may depend on the level of activity in your city, but in Montreal, with the range of my interests, if I tried to do everything I would be attending one or more activities every day. At one point in my life, I basically tried that. After a few months, I was exhausted. Focus on what will have an impact and help you scale your brand. You will miss some stuff, even some crucial stuff, but that's okay.

Tip Think about the list of things you can do as a sky's-the-limit shopping list: you don't have the money to buy everything. You will have to choose, and again, it's about prioritizing and thinking about impact.

Give Away Your Ideas

Since you've learn to say no to yourself (right?), and you don't suffer from FOMO (correct?), share your ideas. I'm not talking about giving away all your ideas—just the ones you don't have time to do or don't have the time or interest to maintain anymore.

I told you about the Festival Geek de Montréal; someone else took the lead on it, and they are continuing the tradition—and I won't be part of the organization. I was not always focused, and back then I was starting up any idea I had. Even if they were good ideas and helped me in one way or another, they were not always related to my brand or goal. Another project I started three years ago was FailCampMtl (Fail Camp Montréal). It was more of a small conference than a real camp/unconference. In one evening, I had four speakers sharing failures they had experienced in their lives, on the personal side or related to their career. The idea was not to laugh at them, but to be proud of them, because they were courageous enough to share their embarrassing moments with others and learn from their failures. I'm a huge believer that failure is not the end—you can learn from it. So the event was all about that. I was happy, as I got a full house on the first event (79 persons, the maximum for the room). Thanks to my speakers, it went well, and people were totally inspired.

It was a great event; I had fun organizing it, and people were asking for another. But it did not happen. At least, not with me at the helm. Even though it hadn't taken much time to create this small event, it was still taking time that I could use to do something else that would be more related to my brand. So I decided to do a blog post to announce I wouldn't be doing another edition, but would be more than happy to give it to someone. Within one day I got a comment from someone who wanted to take on the project. He and his team produced the second edition, and from what I hear, it was a real success. By giving the project away, I gave the attendees what they wanted: a second event. On top of that, now the new leader can claim he organizes it, and that claim did not remove my title of founder. No matter who runs the event in 10 years, or if the event stop never makes it to year three, I will always be the one who created it, and the new leader will be the one who saved it. Giving your ideas to others helps you focus on what makes sense, and you still get to see those ideas becoming projects.

You Don't Know Everything, and It's Okay

When I was volunteering for the Boy Scouts, I was training the other volunteers—the ones that would be with the kids. One piece of advice I gave was to never lie to a child. It's okay to say you don't know something. Their role as adults in that organization is to help kids be better citizens, and lying to them doesn't do that. At that age, kids have a lot of questions, and they were asking their leaders (my trainees) a ton of them. My advice was that if one kid asks you a question you don't know the answer to, say you don't know but will try to find out. It's better to tell them you don't know than to invent an answer or tell them something you're not sure of and that may not be true. It would break your connection, and the trust they have in you, if they found out you were lying to them. I give the same advice to people who start public speaking, and I will give you the same advice for your personal brand: don't lie. It's okay not to know everything, even if it's in your area of expertise.

When you say or write something, be sure about it. As I've mentioned, everything you will say or write can be held against you. On top of that, your credibility may suffer if you say something wrong. Know your stuff! You are the expert, so act like it.

Give Your Time

You need to learn to say no, but you shouldn't *always* say no. There are many ways to give your time. Let's start with volunteering. It's perfect for someone who doesn't have any experience, as it's an interesting way to get some. It's not paid work, but you have the chance to do stuff related to your industry, meet new people, and do some social good. There are many organizations that help adults and kids learn programming, so you could use your skills to help them. It's something you can put on your résumé, but the reward is way bigger than putting the experience on your LinkedIn profile: what you get from the attendees is quite often fantastic.

You could volunteer for something totally unrelated to your domain of expertise. Volunteering in the Boy Scouts for 11 years gave me a lot more than I gave to them. It taught me responsibility, how to be a better citizen, and how to harvest my leadership skills. It helped me find my love of sharing my passion in front of people, and a lot more. I rarely had to use my computer skills, but it helped me develop soft skills that are important to being a developer—like being responsible, working with others, explaining concepts, and more. It also helped me grow my network, and it was useful when I was a freelancer. It's good to hang with the people in the tech industry, but often those who need your services are not involved in technology.

It's hard for me now to commit to recurring stuff like I used to, but there are other ways to give your time and help others periodically. People often ask me for advice about their startups, companies, business offers, career paths, and applications they are developing. When I have the time to do it (most of the time I do), I happily answer them. I don't hold the ultimate truth of all things, of course, but if my experience can help them, or at least give them another point of view, I'm more than happy to offer it. Does it give me something in return? From a purely economic point of view, no, but it rewards me in other ways. Of course, my first goal is to help people. If you dig a bit deeper, you'll see that by helping others, you set the bar with those relationships. It doesn't mean you have to ask them for something at some point, but if that happens, you can be sure they will return the favor (or most of them will). You may also take that relationship to the next level: customers or colleagues may become friends. Strangers may become acquaintances and part of your network.

I also help developers looking for jobs or companies looking for new team members. I'm not in the headhunting business, but my network is quite interesting, and it's always a pleasure to help those people. It doesn't pan out every time, but at least I'm trying, and most of the time it's not complicated. If I have someone in mind with a particular expertise, I introduce each side to the other and let them work out the rest. More often than not, my direct entourage is not looking for work, so I use my social media channels to publish a status about an amazing new job offer or share a contact who is looking for a new challenge. Both actions take five minutes. When I blogged about looking for a new job after leaving Microsoft, it was the most popular post ever on my blog. My network helps me spread the word as I help them spread their messages.

> **Remember** Even if you're not paid for it, you should respect your commitment—and make Art!

Give Your Time: Part 2

You can give your work instead of giving your time, and in the end, it's kind of the same. I'm not talking about working for free all the time, but it may be useful at some point. A good example would be starting as a freelancer. It can be hard to launch your business and acquire customers if you don't already have a good portfolio to show them. I planned to use that technique to help me get my first customer when I started my company. As I mentioned, I had no iPhone development experience. Nevertheless, I contacted one of the most famous technology bloggers in Montreal and proposed creating an iPhone app for him that would give his readers an interactive way to read his blog, tweets, and more, by thinking about offline. At that time, it was not like today; offline application was mostly something you were able to achieve with native development (Objective-C for iOS, .NET for Windows Phone, Java for BlackBerry, and so on).

I don't remember if the deal was to do it for free or very cheap, but in either case, I would be losing money. The idea was simple. First, it would give me experience creating an iPhone app. Then I would finally be able to show customers one app I made, which would be available in the App Store. Some customers wanted to see the code. I don't know why (they didn't know how to code), but I would have been able to do so with this app. Last but not least, I would be able to add this superstar blogger to my list of customers. People didn't have to know that I did it for free or cheap. Because so many people would be reading his blog, any percentage who used the app would be significant, and the app being promoted on his site would provide some good visibility for me. Any way you looked at it, it was a good deal for both of us. (In the end,

I never did the app because I got a customer before we concluded a deal, and when the blogger finally decided to go with his app, I had left the unemployed world for my first job as an evangelist. No worries for this prospect: I put him in contact with one of the best iPhone developers in the city.)

Of course, it's usually not a pleasant experience to fail at something. We put in so much energy and passion. Why did our project fail? Why did it happen to us? It's no fun, but it's not the end. Failure is an opportunity to learn from your mistakes. That's why I created FailCampMtl—I wanted people to understand this important concept. One of the principles of lean startup methodology is: fail, but fail fast. You may not succeed the first time with your brand. You may try some of the suggestions in this book, and they may not work for you. In any case, if you fail, learn from it and go to the next step in your plan. Don't take it too personally; continue your journey. As the saying goes, you can't make the same mistake twice. The second time you make it, it's a choice!

A/S/L?

Maybe you're too young to recall the era of Internet Relay Chat (IRC). Even for those who still use it today, IRC is nothing like it was in its heyday. When I was younger, I was on IRC all the time, spending time with cyberfriends, real friends, and people I did not know at all. I was always looking for someone interesting to talk to and, let's be honest, some ladies, too (I was super shy until I was 19). Even before texting, we were using abbreviations. A/S/L stands for age, sex, location. It was often the first question asked when chatting on IRC because usually you had no idea who was online. Nicknames might give you an idea, but mostly the Internet was a place full of anonymous people.

Normally, you did not expose private information or divulge your identity on the Internet. Everything was anonymous. The Internet was new, and we were afraid of people finding out where we lived or trying to steal from us. Of course, we know the web a lot better now—those dangers are still present, but we know how to manage them better. But anonymity isn't what it used to be. Real identities are mostly known now online. Of course, you are building a brand about you, so you need to be yourself on the web. Be you.

What does that mean? First, use your real name when you sign something or create an account somewhere. It will help people find you on those services or websites and will make you visible on Google and other search engines. That means also use your real picture, one of good quality, where people can easily identify you (as much as I like kids and cats, they won't help me identify you in a photo). The era of being anonymous on the web is done. Of course, I'm not talking about the rest of your personal data. You need to keep that safe. But using your real name and a real picture will give you more than it can hurt. Most people are not good with names: a picture will help them identify you. I use a picture of me everywhere I can. On the last slides of all my talks (check out www.slideshare.net/fredericharper to see some), I include a picture of me. It helps people who browse the slides later remember that it was the bald guy from Mozilla that did this talk.

I do the same thing for my business cards (yes, as digital as I can be, business cards are still useful): my face is on them. I do a lot of conferences and networking events, and many people give me their business cards. I remember those I get a card from better than those who don't offer one. I usually talk to lots of people during events, and I have a bad memory for names. I suspect many people are like me; hence, my cards have big face on them.

Being consistent in using your picture (updating it periodically—don't keep the same one for 10 years) helps people remember you, and not just on the web; it happens in real life, too. Often people recognize me at an event because they saw my avatar on Twitter or pictures of me on my blog. They can recognize me because I use a real picture of me. It helps create a link between the virtual world and the real world.

Think about your username, too. Whenever you need a username somewhere, even if you use your real name to create an account, choosing a unique identifier for your profile helps people find you on other sites, including social networks. Most services now try to make their sites or applications social: Yelp, Foursquare, Vivino, MyFitnessPal, Geocaching, Rdio, Untappd, Fitbit, and so on. You can use a tool like NameChk (www.namechk.com) to check the availability of usernames on many sites and applications (see Figure 5-3). At the time of writing, NameChk checks 157 sites at a time.

Chapter 5 | Do Epic Stuff

Figure 5-3. NameChk checks username availability for you

Many years ago, when I decided to go from anonymous to the real Frédéric Harper on the Internet, I had a username that was not particularly unique. I started with fharper. Other people use this username, and quite often it's already in use when I try to register somewhere new (or my memory is worse than I thought, and I have forgotten that I already created an account for those sites). I hate it when that happens, but what I do in those circumstances is use fredericharper. It's a bit too late to change fharper to fredericharper everywhere, as it will confuse people (maybe it's something I should do at some point to be consistent). At least I have fharper on the four most important places for me: my email address, Twitter, GitHub, and Facebook. You don't have to use part of your real name, but it will be easier for people to remember if you do. It will also look better than ilovespongebob16. I could have used my old nickname, as it was unique and well known in my entourage, but by using fharper, it's easier for people to remember. Because it's not easy for many names, my advice is to go full name first, like fredericharper, and see what happens with NameChk. If it's not working, try playing a bit with it like frederic_harper, fredharper, fred_harper, harperfrederic, harperfred, and so on. Try to avoid using numbers if possible, like yourname123. Other possible variants depend on your name and what you want.

Remember   Your name is your brand.

If You're Not on Google, You Don't Exist

I received no money from Google for this section.[1] No matter your technology affiliation or religion, Google is still the most used search engine out there.

My point here is simple: if you're not on Google, you do not exist. If I look up your name on Google and find nothing about you, you don't exist on the web. If you've never done it, open a browser in private mode, which doesn't use your preferences, search history, or cookies. By using a "clean" browser, your search result won't be affected and you will see "normal" results. Go to Google (or your preferred search engine—though you should use Google whether you like it or not because it's the most popular engine) and type your full name. What are the results? Are they about you or someone else? Are they mixed results? Do the results lead to the sites you would like them

---

[1] Full disclosure: Google is a YulDev+ sponsor for my YulDev group (http://yuldev.ca) and was one of the sponsors for HTML5mtl (http://html5mtl.ca) when I co-founded the group with Mathieu Chartier and Benoit Piette.

to? Don't bother looking after the first page of results, unless you don't find what you're looking for on the first one and want to know where it stands compared to the other links. Most users never go beyond the first page. Let's take a look at my own results, shown in Figure 5-4.

Figure 5-4. The first page of the search result for Frédéric Harper on Google

My results are quite good: you can see my blog, pictures of me, articles I wrote, and more. It seems there is another Frederic Harper (without the accented letters) who has a good presence on the web, too, but he's a painter, so our worlds don't collide that much. With the nature of my brand and job, I have a bigger presence online, too (sorry, Fred!). One thing I don't like is that Twitter and LinkedIn rank higher than my blog, which is in third position. That's why I ask people to point to my blog instead of Twitter or LinkedIn.

You need to work on your online presence—and we'll see which tools you can use to be there—to exist on Google and monitor what is going on with you on the web in Chapter 6.

Content Is King

That heading is not wholly accurate; *good* content is king. You probably understand that personal branding is a lot about content: content you create, content you share, content you don't share, content you talk about, content you write, and so on. Chapter 6 covers how to create content, how to share it, and how to be sure it gets the visibility it deserves.

There are many ways to create content and many tools available to help you. Content is often text, though not always. Creating content is something you can learn with time and experience. I'm not talking about just making noise by posting on your blog all the time, or tweeting everything that pops in your head. I'm talking about useful, high-quality content. It doesn't have to be unique; you don't have to be the first one to say it. You just need to have an idea or an opinion to share—something that is yours. Keep that in mind when you read Chapter 6.

Educate Yourself

You should never stop learning. I'm not talking about going back to school, because there are many other ways to learn. Content is king in both directions: you create it and you consume it. Of course, it's not always easy to find the right content, and much of it is not valuable. The web shouldn't be your only source of content: it depends on what you're looking for, which media you like, and how you learn best.

Personally, I have two sources of content from which I educate myself on various topics, get news about the world, and help me stay informed of what is happening in the industry. I mainly get my information from RSS feeds, either from news sites or different blogs. (Blogs are an endless source of valuable information if they're well curated.) The second way to get information is books. It's probably that way for you, too—after all, you're reading this one. I don't read paper versions of books very often anymore: I prefer to get the digital versions. It's easier for me to read any book, at any moment, as long as my reading device is charged. I'm also reading, or should I say, listening, to audio books. I recommend a few relevant books in Chapter 8.

You Have a Limited Number of Keystrokes

I took this idea from a blog post by Scott Hanselman (www.hanselman.com/blog/DoTheyDeserveTheGiftOfYourKeystrokes.aspx), that we have a limited number of hours in our life, and a limited number of keystrokes. It relates to the importance of impact and how you want to have scalability in what you do.

People often ask me questions, mostly by email. They range from advice on how to be a technical evangelist, to where to start to become a web developer, to the best user groups in Montreal for people interested in startups. If the question is not private, and the answer could help more than one person, I write a blog post, publish it, and send the link to the person. I make sure to respect the asker's privacy. This method helps me reach more people. Often people ask me a question related to a blog post I already wrote, so I only have to point them to the post. That way, I help the person who asked the question, I give some of my time and expertise (but also save time by simply pointing them to something I already did), and am able to scale by reaching more people. In the end, it takes about the same amount of time to write a blog post as it does to write an email (okay, I always try to find amazing images to add to the post, so it does take a bit longer). Even so, if you take the time it took you to blog and divide it by the number of people who benefit from your post, that number will always be smaller than dividing by the one person who would have received an email reply. Think about it, and save your keystrokes.

Don't Be a Sheep

I said your brand doesn't have to be about something unique or very niche, and I want to be sure you understand that point. People often tell me they can't work on the brand they would like to work on because there is already a superstar in their domain. But think about this: if we did not do stuff simply because somebody else is doing it, we would have only one grocery store per city, only one lawyer in your town, and only one company offering web development. There is enough audience for everyone, and you will always have your own personal touch and expertise.

Think about me: being a technical evangelist about web technologies is far from being unique. There are four in my company alone. On the other hand, I have my own unique style that you know by now. It's the same for you. Maybe there is another superstar using Python like no one else in your company. That's okay. Maybe you'll differentiate yourself by being the one who masters integration with mobile platforms.

You need to look to others and take away good tricks you can reuse (my idea to record my presentations was inspired by a colleague). But use your head—you don't want to be a copycat, either.

A Small Guide to Losing Your Shyness

I was talking about this book with my friend Fabrice Calando a couple of weeks ago at a local startup event.[2] He said (I'm paraphrasing), "Great idea, Fred, but what about shy people? It won't be as easy for them to execute your advice as it was for you." Fair enough. Most of the stuff in this book can be done behind a screen, from the comforting protection of your computer, but let's agree on the fact that the part that happens on the Outernet is impactful and critical to your success. What happens if you are shy or introverted?

A couple of years ago, I was one of the shyest people on Earth. Talking to someone—for example, my teacher—was torture. It gave me stomach pains, and it was quite a challenge. I don't know why, because I've always liked people, but I was really shy. Some years ago I decided to change. I had had enough! Enough of missing opportunities, enough of feeling like I was climbing Mount Everest every time I had to do something out of my small comfort zone. It was the beginning of a new life, the beginning of a journey where I had no limits on doing what I wanted. I'm quite happy with my life now, the one I built with this new Fred, the one who is not shy anymore.

If you're shy, how you can do the same thing? To be honest, I don't remember how I made this change. I went from being very shy to having no problem getting up on the table and dancing. Maybe I've gone too far toward the extrovert end of the scale, but you get the point. What I do remember is that *forced* myself to go out of my comfort zone (all roads don't lead to Rome, they all lead outside your comfort zone). I *challenged* myself to talk to new people. I gave myself permission to fail. I stopped caring about what others would think about me. I started to do things that would help me silence my shyness. It helped me shape the person I am today.

---

[2]Fabrice is one of the most brilliant people I know (you should read his blog at http://fabricecalando.com). It's mostly about marketing, but a lot about just being better in your everyday life.

I'm no psychological expert, but I have nothing against helping you with a little recipe of mine. Here is my plan for you. It may sound silly at first, but it will help you to get out of your comfort zone (or should I say, out of your shy zone).

1. **In a public place, start a conversation with a stranger.** Start with small talk. Something as simple as "How are you today? The weather is amazing! Have a good day." It will be a great first step, but don't stop there. Do this as often as you feel comfortable doing it without a lot of mental preparation.

2. **At the coffee shop, pay for someone else's order.** It's a random act of kindness. In today's world, your beneficiary may become perplexed and try to find out if you have a hidden agenda. You'll see that this act is harder than you think, but it can help you to do something unusual like this. The price of a coffee is not too big to help you achieve more. If it wasn't easy the first time you did this, do it more often. Do it as often as you need to become comfortable doing so.

3. **When coming back from work or school, instead of walking on the sidewalk, dance.** Yes, move yourself from point A to point B by dancing. It's okay if you don't know how to dance; I don't know either, but that's not really the point. Just yesterday, I did this because the music I was listening to was energetic, and I was happy. It made people smile, and hopefully, my happiness became contagious. Maybe some of them laughed at me. I don't care. Nobody died, and it was not the end of the world.

4. **Take a friend to a karaoke bar and sing.** Don't choose one with a private room—go to one where you sing in front of everybody. Yes, I'm asking you to sing. Personally, I love karaoke, even if I sing like the living dead (do they even sing?). Choose a song you know well and go for it. Guess what? Nobody in the room is a professional singer. Karaoke can also help you get out of your comfort zone and you will have a wonderful evening with friends.

5. **Ask the leader of a local user group for permission to speak for one minute before the beginning of the main presentation.** Share a cool framework or project. Most user groups provide an opportunity for this. Sixty seconds may sound short, but trust me, once you're up there it will seem like an eternity. You can also do this at work. Ask your manager for one minute at the next team meeting or lunch. If you've already talked to a stranger, danced on the sidewalk, and sang in a karaoke bar, you can handle this like a champion.

Those exercises have two goals. First, they can help you minimize your stress while talking to people (or in front of people). And they can make you realize that you will never look like a fool, no matter what you do, if you don't *think* you look like one. Your fear is all in your head. If you get through my list, don't stop there. Come up with your own exercises for reducing social fear.

Of course, your shyness won't magically go away after you do these exercises. The idea is to set the stage. It's the appetizer before a bigger meal—meant to work up your appetite to do more of those things. As with everything else, the more you do a thing that scares you, the less it will scare you. The first time I talked to a stranger in a coffee shop, I was scared. The first time I spoke in front a crowd at school, I thought I was going to die. I won't even tell you about my first presentation in English as it's not my mother tongue. It was the same thing every time: doing something new that was challenging the part saying I couldn't do it, that I was too shy. Get over your fear of what others think. Jump in with both feet. You won't die, and you will be proud of what you will achieve.

Do you feel everything coming together? In Chapter 6, you will learn more about how to take these concepts and work on your brand with specific actions. You will learn about tools, services, and websites you can use to get more visibility, show your expertise, grow your network, scale, and have a real impact.

CHAPTER 6

Weapons of Choice
The How, Part 2

If you do what you've always done, you'll get what you've always gotten.

—Tony Robbins

I start each chapter with a testimonial about personal branding from someone else in the industry. Maybe you know this leader for his nickname, the "Godfather of Web Standards." Maybe you know him for his podcast, the Big Web Show (www.muleradio.net/thebigwebshow/)? Perhaps you follow his Web magazine, which started as a mailing list, A List Apart (http://alistapart.com)? Or maybe you know the publishing company A Book Apart (www.abookapart.com), which he co-founded with Mandy Brown and Jason Santa Maria? If you're in the Web industry, perhaps you know him for the conference series he started with Eric Meyer, called An Event Apart (http://aneventapart.com)? Or from his web design and development shop, Happy Cog (http://happycog.com)? I could continue this list for a long time. One of the reasons I'm so happy to have Jeffrey Zeldman's thoughts on personal branding is that he is a doer—he puts his money where his mouth is.[1] This chapter is all about concrete stuff.

---

[1] Jeffrey has a podcast, the Big Web Show (www.muleradio.net/thebigwebshow/); a web magazine, which started as a mailing list, A List Apart (http://alistapart.com); and a publishing company, A Book Apart (www.abookapart.com), which he co-founded with Mandy Brown and Jason Santa Maria. He also started conference series with Eric Meyer, called An Event Apart (http://aneventapart.com). His web design and development shop is called Happy Cog (http://happycog.com).

Chapter 6 | Weapons of Choice

Jeffrey told me why he thinks personal branding is important for a developer:

> There are a million people who can code a web page, a million who can design one. So why do so many of the best jobs fall to just a handful of well-known designers and developers? The question answers itself. The best gigs go to the best-known practitioners like the best acting jobs go to the biggest stars. Designers have known this for years. Attending a graphic design conference is essentially like watching a series of portfolio reviews. As opposed to a web design conference, where the lecturer tries to convey a concept or explain a method of working, speakers at graphic design conferences just show their work and talk about their famous clients. You wonder why hard-working designers pony up hundreds or thousands of dollars to attend a conference like that. But they do. They find it inspiring. All designers dream of being Paul Rand, of designing the IBM logo. Successful web designers and developers seem to do the same.

It's all about differentiating yourself, and as Jeffrey said, there are many people capable of doing the same job. Clearly not everybody will be successful.

I was looking forward to his response to how personal branding helped his career, because he has a huge personal brand:

> I started calling myself "Zeldman" (not using my first name) 15 years before I was @zeldman on Twitter. I had noticed that single names were powerful. Think of Cher or Prince. There was a jazz guy I admired named Joseph Zawinul. When he played with Miles Davis, he used his full name. But once he started his own band (Weather Report), he just went by his last name: Zawinul.

> Everyone else on his records had a first and last name, from Wayne Shorter to Jaco Pastorius and beyond. But Zawinul was just Zawinul. That made him not just a great player but also a great brand. Brian Eno did the same thing for quite a while. He was just Eno.

> These were musicians (or, in Eno's case, nonmusicians) I grew up listening to, admiring, and trying pathetically to emulate. (I used to be in music.) I noticed what they did, and I copied it.

> I was also influenced by my favorite filmmaker, Alfred Hitchcock. He wasn't a single name. But he got his name above the title at a time when that was pretty well unheard of. (A couple of other auteur directors achieved this status as well; Hitch wasn't the only one.) Later, in the early days of TV, Hitchcock lent his name to a 30-minute melodrama ("Alfred Hitchcock Presents") which featured different stories and characters every week; as host, Hitchcock introduced each episode using a droll style that made him a beloved figure and household name.

> He didn't do all this stuff to become famous. He did it because, as a brand, as a name above the title, he had more power and was able to hew closer to his artistic vision.
>
> And that's the same reason Zawinul and Eno made brands of themselves.
>
> It sounds yucky to talk about this kind of thing. It's even faintly embarrassing. But if you care about your work and want to do the best work possible, you need to have a great career. And to have a great career, you need power. The more of brand-name designer or developer you can become, the more leverage you will acquire over the work, and the less often you'll be forced to design or develop things you don't believe in, for people you don't respect.

I like the approach in this answer: you might expect an answer about himself, but instead it's mostly about who inspired him. As you already know, personal branding isn't just for developers or designers, it's for everyone. It's also not just about being famous or obtaining power, but achieving your end goals, such as developing the projects or applications you believe in with people you respect.

Last, but not least, Jeffrey offers some advice on how to reach the next goal in your career.

> In spite of what I've just said, never think about how well known you are. Never compare yourself to others. ("Compare and despair.") The best way to achieve "fame" in our field and to become a brand name is to do work on behalf of the community and give it away free. How did Dave Shea become Dave Shea? By creating CSS Zen Garden for the benefit of developers and designers everywhere. And the new generation of rising stars like Jenn Lukas and superstars like Chris Coyier have followed the same path. Jenn empowers women to become front-end developers. She does it because she cares. In the process, she becomes well known. Chris Coyier creates tools and publications that improve CSS and the lot of the CSS practitioner. He does this because he genuinely cares about the industry and is honestly excited to work with this technology. He doesn't do it to become famous. He does it for the love of it. And the community loves him back.
>
> My advice is to give, do service, make what's missing. Don't see the kind of web magazine or web tool you'd like to see? Make it yourself. As one benefit, you'll have access to a great tool. As another, you'll get known (and loved) and people will think of you when they have a gig.

When people reach that level of credibility, we trust them, which is why I'm glad Jeffrey gave us that advice: he couldn't be more right. No matter what your end goal is, you'll have a bigger impact than you think. I remember the first time I met Jeffrey in 2012. It was at Go Beyond Pixels (http://gobeyondpixels.com), a conference created by Levin Mejia in St. John's, Newfoundland and Labrador, Canada. At the time, I was a technical evangelist at Microsoft, and I was thrilled to share the stage at a conference with a big name like him. After my presentation, during the break, Jeffrey came to see me and told me that my presentation was great and that I had done a great job. I'll always remember the scene. I was with a friend and colleague at that time, Thomas Lewis. I turned toward him and asked if I was dreaming or if Jeffrey said what I thought he just said. Thomas, also a fan of Jeffrey's work, confirmed that it happened. I'm not a groupie kind of person, but having someone like him tell me that I did a great job was amazing.

By taking the time to come talk to someone he didn't know and telling me I did a great job, Jeffrey helped me a lot. My role was changing at the time, and I was having trouble finding my way. His gentle words comforted me. They offered me a different view on the situation and helped me line up the next couple of months to fix my issues and find a good path for me.

By the phrase *weapons of choice*, I'm alluding to Christopher Walken in the Fatboy Slim music video for "Weapon of Choice" (www.youtube.com/watch?v=XQ7z57qrZU8). If you've never seen this video, you need to watch it. Did you see how Christopher Walken seems to have fun making this video? Of course, it's his job to act, but did you feel the pleasure he had? The man loves what he's doing. You have to choose the tools, or weapons, you'll use to make your brand a reality—and if you have no fun, it won't work.

In this chapter, I share with you, in no particular order, some of the tools I'm using. Some I've used for a long time, some are newer, and some I'm only beginning to use. I want to give you tools I know are working while opening your mind to new ones that may be useful. Choose the ones that make sense for you and for your brand, ones that you can prioritize to get a tremendous impact. Use your common sense, and let's see how you can make your brand a reality.

What about the stuff you don't know? As Tony Robbins said, "If you do what you've always done, you'll get what you've always gotten." Remember the section in Chapter 5 about getting out of your comfort zone? You'll try new tools you've never used or didn't even know about, and that's okay. Do you want different results? You need different tools. It doesn't mean that what you do right now isn't good, but you need to see what can help you get from point A to point B. Ready? Let's continue this journey.

I Blog, You Blog, We All Blog

If there's one thing you need to start doing now, it's blogging. As you surely know, a blog is a website where you post articles about your topic(s) of choice. It's focused on discussion and often includes a comment section. Blogging is a good way to have an online presence on the Internet and get the search engines to admit that you exist.

Tip You really need a blog. The main goal of starting a blog is to help you with your brand. But it also gives you a presence on the Internet that you own and provides a platform to show your expertise—and perhaps become known for it.

Owning Your Content

As much as I like and recommend social media (covered in Chapter 7), you're not the owner of the platform—and quite often you don't even own your profile or the data you add. Social media websites have policies that you must follow, and let's be honest: you probably never took the time to read them (I need to be better at this, too). Because it's their platform, there's very little to stop them from doing what they want (it's a bit more complex than that, but you get the point), such as closing your account.

There are many horror stories about that, but just recently Instagram closed the account of a mom (www.theguardian.com/technology/2014/jun/25/instagram-delete-account-baby-photos-reinstate) named Courtney Adamo. She posted a picture of her baby that didn't comply with the policy of the service. She didn't do it on purpose. Even after reading the policy again, she was convinced she hadn't broken the guidelines. After some noise from the media, Instagram recognized that it had made a mistake and restored her account.

This story had a happy ending, as she got her account back. She didn't lose the last few years of good posts and comments from her friends and family. But it could have ended differently: Instagram could have refused to reactivate her account, and if she hadn't made backups (have you?), she would have lost years of good memories. What would happen if, tomorrow, the social media site you use dramatically changed its policies? What if they closed your account, no matter whether you deserved it? You would lose your content and all your effort. This is why I'm starting this chapter with blogging: by blogging, you own your content.

Showing Your Expertise

Of course, there are many ways to show your expertise to others—employers and future customers—and blogging is one of the best ways. By writing your opinion about a topic, showing some code examples, or explaining how you solve a technical issue at work, you show others that you have that expertise. This is a way to share your thoughts and show you're working with cutting-edge technology (if it's the case)—and that you know how to use it.

In all the job interviews I've ever had, I used my blog as one of my main references in my résumé. First, the blog will give the potential employer or prospect an idea of my knowledge. Even if I don't write a lot of technical posts on my personal blog, I do elsewhere: I was writing my technical posts for my employer's blogs. Since I share my thoughts about many topics, and sometimes just about life, the blog can give future coworkers a good idea of my personality. When I was hiring people, the personality of the developer was as important (if not more so) than technical skills. The blog has helped me build an audience, but I'll come back to that later.

Collateral Benefits

Besides the two advantages discussed so far, there are also collateral benefits of having a blog:

1. It improves your writing skills. (I can imagine the face of my editor right now. Yes, it was worse than this before. Hey, I learned English three years ago!)
2. It helps synthesize your thoughts.

We are developers, not writers, but having good writing skills will help you in every job you'll hold. Like anything else in life, you get better with practice, so the more you write, the better you'll be. It's that simple.

Sometimes you don't know how to write what's in your mind. Sometimes you're not sure whether others will get your point. Sometimes it's not even clear in your own head, so how can it be clear when you share it with others? Writing helps synthesize, or bring together, your thoughts.

If those points didn't convince you, nothing will. So let's see where you can start blogging.

How to Start Blogging

First, you need to decide if you want to use an online blog service or host it on your own server. There are many free services online, such as Wordpress (https://wordpress.com), Tumblr (www.tumblr.com), Typepad (www.typepad.com), Ghost (https://ghost.org), and Medium (https://medium.com). With a free service, you don't have to pay for your hosting solution, unless you want premium features. It's a good way to get started because you don't have to invest a dime, and it's as easy as can be.

■ **Warning**   One thing about free blog services is that, most of the time, you have to use their domain name. Eventually, you'll probably want your own domain name, which I strongly suggest for your brand.

Now let's say you want to host your own blog on your own website (which I suggest because it's how you will totally own your content). You'll still need to choose which blogging platform you want to use. There are many possibilities, from a blogging platform like Wordpress, to CMS (content management system) like Drupal (many people use CMS as a blogging platform), to a static site generator (an engine that converts to a static HTML site—no more databases or content generated on the fly) like Jekyll, which some people (mostly developers) use to blog. Some are easy, like most blogging platforms, and others are more complex, like static site generators; some are very minimal, like Ghost, and most have features that you'll never use, like most CMS platforms. With Jekyll (http://jekyllrb.com), Drupal (www.drupal.org), Ghost (https://ghost.org/), Pelican (http://blog.getpelican.com/), and the well-known Wordpress (http://wordpress.org/), you can host your own version, or use their online service (hence the different sites wordpress.com and wordpress.org).

I've been using Wordpress for more than nine years now. It is still the leading blogging platform out there with more than 60 million websites using it. It's easy to use and gives you access to simple customization with various themes and plugins. I'm a developer, and although I can code everything I want, I like the simplicity of just being able to blog when I need to blog.

The starting procedure is mostly the same for all platforms, including Wordpress. You'll need a website hosting provider, if you don't already have one. You won't need a lot of resources (CPU, memory, hard disk space), especially at the beginning, since you won't have many readers. You'll also need a domain. Many registrars are available where you can buy a domain name for an average of $10/year, depending on the name.

Detailed instructions on starting a blog are beyond the scope of this book, and there is plenty of good documentation online. The Wordpress documentation (http://codex.wordpress.org/Getting_Started_with_WordPress) is a good example. The bottom line: for less than $100 a year and not too much effort, you can have your own blog, with your own domain name. It is worth the investment. My blog brings me a lot, and will probably continue to do so.

Finally, you want to choose your editorial line: what will you talk about? The experts will tell you to find one topic and write about it. To some extent, I agree, as it will help narrow your expertise and focus on your brand. But remember, the goal here is to start a blog to *promote your own brand*. On my blog, I talk about anything I want: technical stuff, personal ideas, web technology, projects I have, songs I like, projects from my friends, and so on. It's my platform. I do what I want with it, and you should, too.

Tip If you don't think you'll have the time to create a blog yourself, you can always start by writing for your company's blog or starting one for your enterprise. In that case, you won't own your content, and you don't have as much as power as you might like, but it's a good way to start and see if you like it. I do both because blogging is part of my job: I've blogged and still blog on employers' sites like the hacks blog (https://hacks.mozilla.org/) at Mozilla, but I'm always writing for my personal blog, too. I highly suggest starting your own blog as well. I know some people in the industry doing some amazing things and becoming well known, but the credit for their work goes only to the enterprise. What happens when they leave the company?

What to Expect from Your Blog

Now you have your blog, and you've started to write some posts. What should you expect? Like anything else, you can't expect it to take off immediately after your first post: it's a journey you just started. It takes time to get readers, and even more time to get quality commenters. Be patient. I've blogged for nine years, and it has taken that long to get where I am now. My blog (shown in Figure 6-1) proved useful in landing some jobs, and it got me the book offers I mentioned in Chapter 5. The publishers found my name by searching different topics and then saw some articles I wrote.

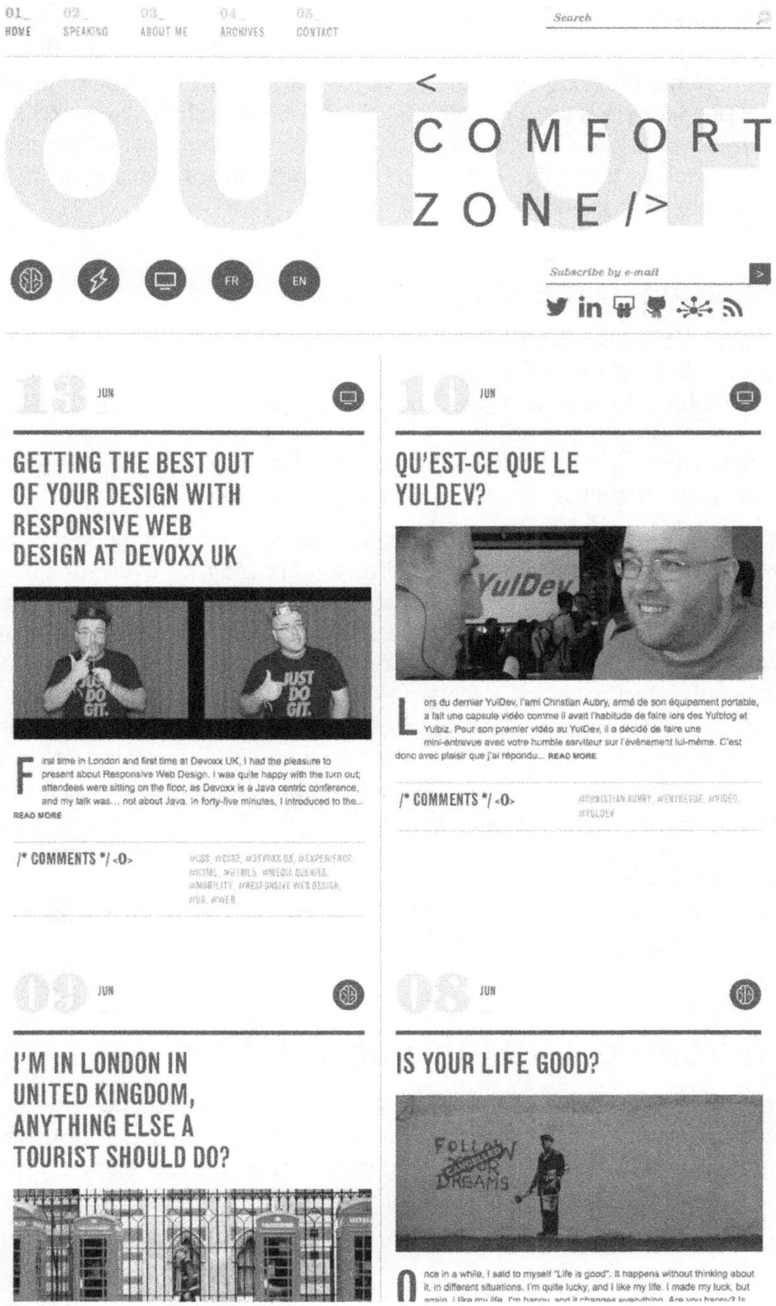

Figure 6-1. This is my home on the Internet, my blog (note the topical variety; http://outofcomfortzone.net)

Blog for yourself first—have fun sharing your passion. Reserve some time during your week to blog, and write as much as you like. Experts will say you should maintain a blogging schedule or write a minimum number of posts per month or per week. Personally, I blog when I have something I want to share. I tried to do so on a regular schedule, but the fun of it was lost when I did that. So now I'm back to blogging whenever I have something I really want to write about or share with the web.

Participating in the Blogosphere

One thing you can also do, whether or not you decide to start a blog of your own, is comment on others' blogs. I'm not talking about promoting your stuff or your own blog. I mean entering discussions you find interesting or arguing in a polite way on a topic another blogger wrote about (don't be a troll or start a flame war). Commenting is another good way to gain credibility and get known for your expertise. In any case, stay true to yourself.

There's also guest blogging. That's when you write blog posts elsewhere, as a guest writer on a friend's blog, on another expert blog, or even for an online magazine. The idea is to blog on someone else's property to share about something on which you have expertise. The advantage is mutual: the owner of the blog will get new content for his or her readers, and you'll gain visibility to new people who may not already follow you. Of course, if you have your own blog, you need to find a balance between blogging for another property and writing the posts that will be published on yours. Guest blogging is a frequent practice that many bloggers do, so don't be afraid to ask sites if you can write an article: in the worst case, they will say no. You can also invite people to guest-post on your blog. It's a growth hacking tactic, as often you will find someone with more visibility than you. You can also just find someone with a different point of view or expertise: it will certainly please your readers and may help you grow your readership.

Open Source, GitHub, and the Like

Open source is beneficial for other developers, companies, and the industry, but it's also good for you. By making your code available online or contributing to an open-source project, you will help your brand as a developer.

I've always been a believer in open source, but I'm also pragmatic: I'm using the technology I need to use to make things happen. If I have a choice, I'll develop something open. The problem is that not everyone has that vision, and for my first jobs as a developer, I worked on proprietary projects. I would have preferred not to do so, but I needed those jobs. It's true that I worked on many amazing projects, and some of them were even competing (and winning) against huge companies in different countries. I was and still am proud of what I achieved. The problem was that when I was looking for a new job or talking to a potential customer, I had nothing to show them. I wasn't contributing a lot to open-source projects at that time. I couldn't show the code I had written for proprietary projects, so I had no way, except with technical tests (and I don't think those are efficient or representative of the skills of a developer), to show the interviewer that I was a good developer. I wasn't able to show the products themselves, as some were internal projects for customers who didn't want others to know about them, for fear of losing competitive advantage. If the projects I had worked on were open source, it would have been easier for me to show my expertise.

Of course, it's not always possible to work on open-source projects, and it may depend on your customer or boss. We don't all have the opportunity to choose the projects we work on (isn't that the goal with your personal brand?). When possible, think open. Contribute to open-source projects if you can. A good way to start is to help us with software like Firefox and Firefox OS. Volunteers and paid staff writers have written good documentation (https://developer.mozilla.org/en-US/docs/Introduction) on how to start. It doesn't need to be something big—it can be just fixing a bug you found in a small library you use, for example. There are many more projects like these online.

You can even start your own project, or open actual applications you're building. There are many sites where you can share your code: the old timers like SourceForge (http://sourceforge.net) and CodePlex (www.codeplex.com), some like newer ones like Bitbucket (https://bitbucket.org) and GitLab (https://about.gitlab.com), and then, of course, there's GitHub (https://github.com)—where all the cool kids are.

Some people go as far as to say that GitHub is the new résumé for developers. As you can see from my profile (https://github.com/fharper), I'm not the most active developer, but my work doesn't involve coding all the time now (and I choose not to code like crazy during my spare time—I have other hobbies). Even so, every time I can, I publish something online or contribute to someone else's repository. Despite my love for git (the distributed source code management) and GitHub (the online git repository), I don't think it's the new résumé. I think it's very important to have a profile there (or in another online repository), but I don't believe it can replace a résumé.

Chapter 6 | Weapons of Choice

By using an online service like GitHub, you open yourself to more visibility. With an online presence comes the possibility that new people find out about you. You'll see four important things on every profile's front page:

1. The most popular repositories you created or forked (created a copy in your repository);
2. The repositories from others you've contributed to the most;
3. How many commitments you made in all repositories on GitHub;
4. Your personal details like name, email, number of followers, website (I'm always pointing people to my blog), organizations you're part of, and more.

The first three are what you can show to people when you want to show your technical skills. You have an easy way to send this information: a link to your profile. No need to sign a nondisclosure agreement, no username or password to create, no worries that any customers will be upset—just code and projects to show what you did and, more important, how you did it. The fourth one helps you get the word out about you on GitHub. I have people going to my blog from my GitHub profile and vice versa.

Of course, fixing bugs and doing pull requests on GitHub are ways to contribute to open source. It takes time and skills with the programming languages the project is using. If you don't have that time or expertise, you still can help open-source projects by submitting issues or bugs. In the end, you're a user even before you're a developer. In GitHub, those issues you submitted will appear as a contribution in your profile (see the contributions area on my GitHub profile—https://github.com/fharper).

Today, many projects use GitHub, and many also have their own bug tracker system (even if they're using GitHub for the code repository). At Mozilla, Bugzilla (https://bugzilla.mozilla.org/) is our bug tracker. It's where we and people all over the world fill out bug or feature requests internally for an external product, like Firefox (see Figure 6-2 for my Bugzilla profile).

Success in Programming

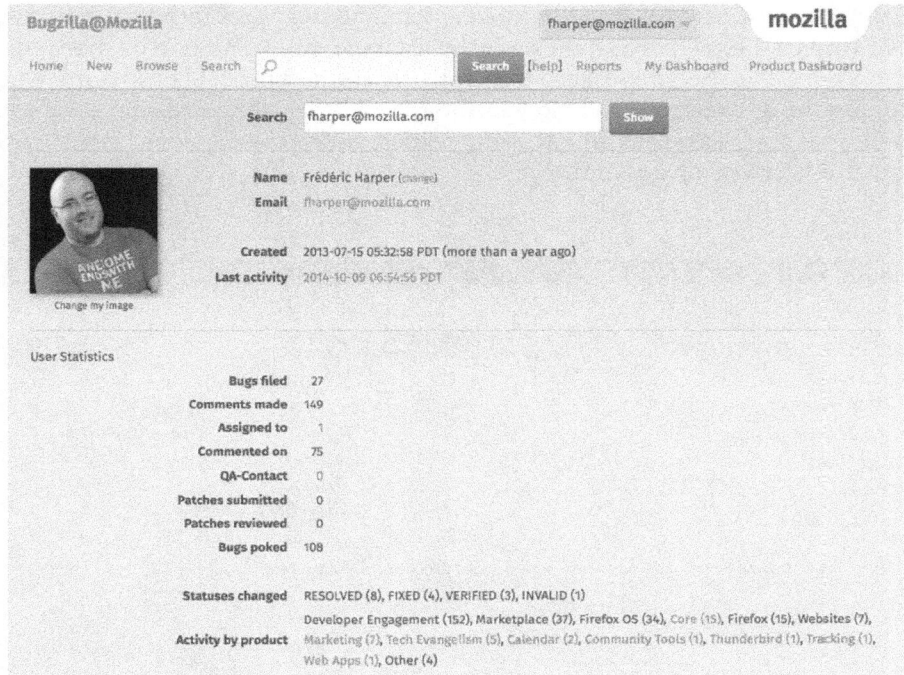

Figure 6-2. My Bugzilla profile

By submitting new bugs, commenting on existing ones, helping solve issues, or doing feature requests, I'm helping the open-source community and those projects grow, even if I didn't fix the code myself. It's another way to build credibility. It shows that I care about the software I use. Even if you can only show a code example by showing your activity report on a tool like Bugzilla or issues you added to GitHub, that's still something you can add to your résumé and be proud of. It will help you solidify your brand.

StackOverflow, How Can I Help You?

StackOverflow (http://stackoverflow.com) is probably one of the most well-known forums for developers out there. It's a resource for developers who are looking for help with their code. Some love it, and some don't. I think it's an amazing resource for developers, but I also agree with some people that it's not well used. Too many developers don't try to understand the proposed solution and just copy-paste it. I guess we are in what I call *the copy-paste era* (I'm guilty of doing it too, once in a while). On the other hand, and the reason I use and love this site, is that many developers have a real issue, have tried to find a solution themselves without success, and reach the point that they need help from their peers.

Chapter 6 | Weapons of Choice

StackOverflow is great if you're looking for an answer to a technical question. No matter the technology, if it's a technical issue, you'll find one or more *tags* (an example is shown in Figure 6-3) you can use, and probably someone who knows the answer and can help you. On top of being a great resource for you and your application, it's an excellent resource for growing your brand. Why not start answering questions?

Figure 6-3. The firefox-os tag on StackOverflow

Success in Programming

You can see my StackOverflow profile in Figure 6-4. What can you conclude about it? I'm far from being one of the most active contributors, but you can see that I'm using my expertise to help other developers. You can also see that I have an interest in everything web, and more important, I provide answers about Firefox OS. As with GitHub, StackOverflow is another way to show your expertise to the rest of the world and help fellow developers in the process. Of course, like anything else, it takes some of your time to answer questions, but it's worth the time.

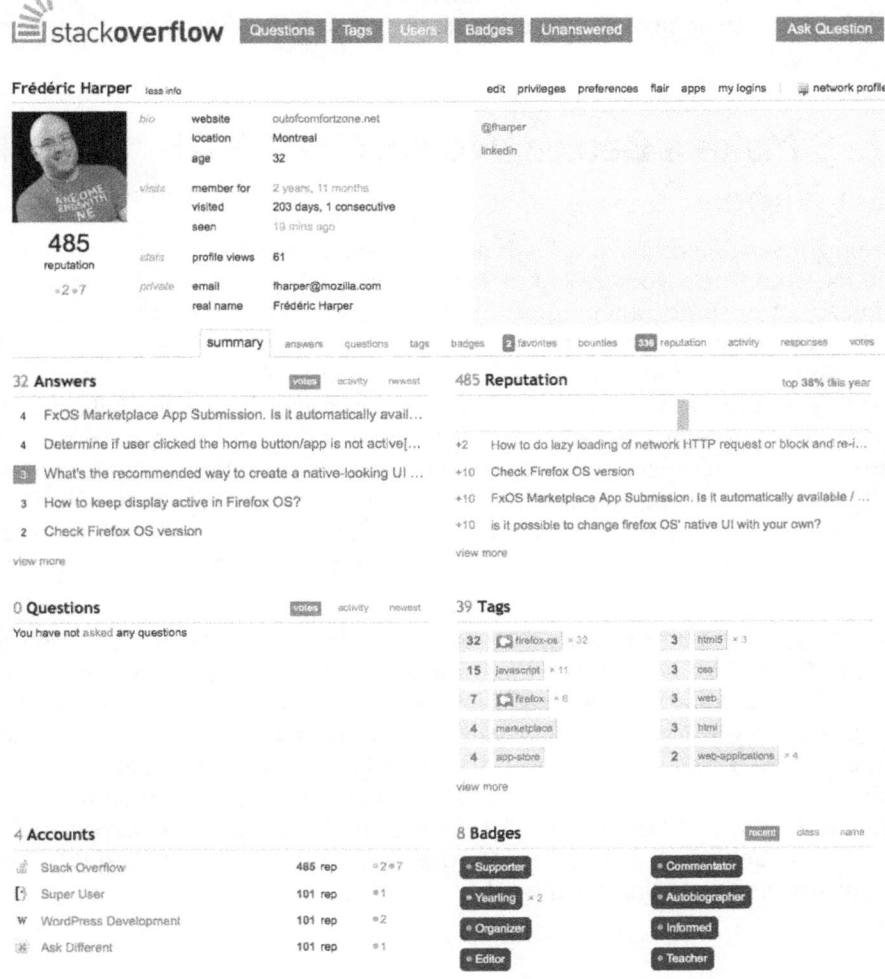

Figure 6-4. My StackOverflow profile

StackOverflow is not all beautiful and shiny. Being part of this community comes with some frustrations. You may have noticed a point system measuring your reputation. I won't explain the magic calculation behind this (StackOverflow provides a quick introduction to the concept at http://stackoverflow.com/tour), but basically, the more you contribute with quality content, the more points you should get. I say *should*, because other users need to approve your answer before you accrue points. One of the irritations of using this site is that many people don't follow up on their questions once they get your answer. Sometimes, you'll answer the question, and even if the answer was right and helped the developer who had the issue, the person who asked it won't take the time to honor your help by accepting your answer. That means fewer points and less recognition for you. But at least you did something good!

Help Make a Better World, One Wiki at a Time

Helping maintain technical wikis is another way to contribute to technology you like—and help your brand in the meantime. If you're a web developer, think about open documentation like Web Platform (http://www.webplatform.org) from the W3C or the Mozilla Developer Network (also known as MDN; https://developer.mozilla.org). Like blogging, this is another way to get better at writing, but it doesn't mean you have to write full articles. There are many ways to help with documentation sites. You can fix a code demo, add a missing sentence to help people understand how to use a new API, or create new documentation that is missing: technology moves so fast, it's not always easy to keep up with. Like the sites I showed you before, some of these have a public profile, so you can brag about what you did (I mean, show your expertise!).

I guess I should add "do as I say, not as I do" here, because I didn't contribute a lot to MDN. The writing team and volunteers working on Firefox OS documentation are doing an amazing job. I decided not to write full articles, but I fix things when I see errors and supplying missing information. By having a profile there (Figure 6-5), I give others a chance to find me and see what I did. I've only contributed to one page so far, but if I had done more, you would have been able to see, like with StackOverflow or Bugzilla, that I have expertise in the topics I helped with. Again, it's another way to show expertise to the rest of the world while doing good work.

Success in Programming

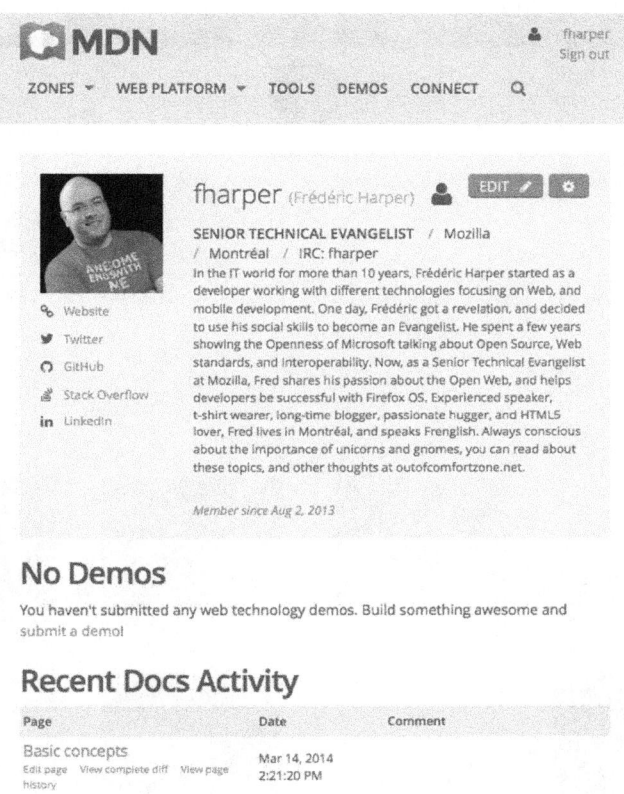

Figure 6-5. My Mozilla Developer Network profile

Show Your Design Skills with Dribbble

If you're like me, you're not great when it comes to design, but many developers (and of course designers) create awesome user interfaces (UIs). One of the tools to create a portfolio and showcase what you've done and what you're working on is Dribbble (https://dribbble.com).

Figure 6-6 shows an example of Lea Verou's Dribbble profile (https://dribbble.com/LeaVerou). She is always developing visually appealing sites and projects. As with all sites mentioned so far, Dribbble offers a social environment. If I were looking for a designer, I would want to see what she or he visually did. Even better, I would love to see some great UI examples. Remember, it will be too late to start a portfolio when you need one to show immediately. When you need to, you can just send a link to your Dribbble account. There are many other sites like this, but Dribbble is one of the most useful.

Chapter 6 | Weapons of Choice

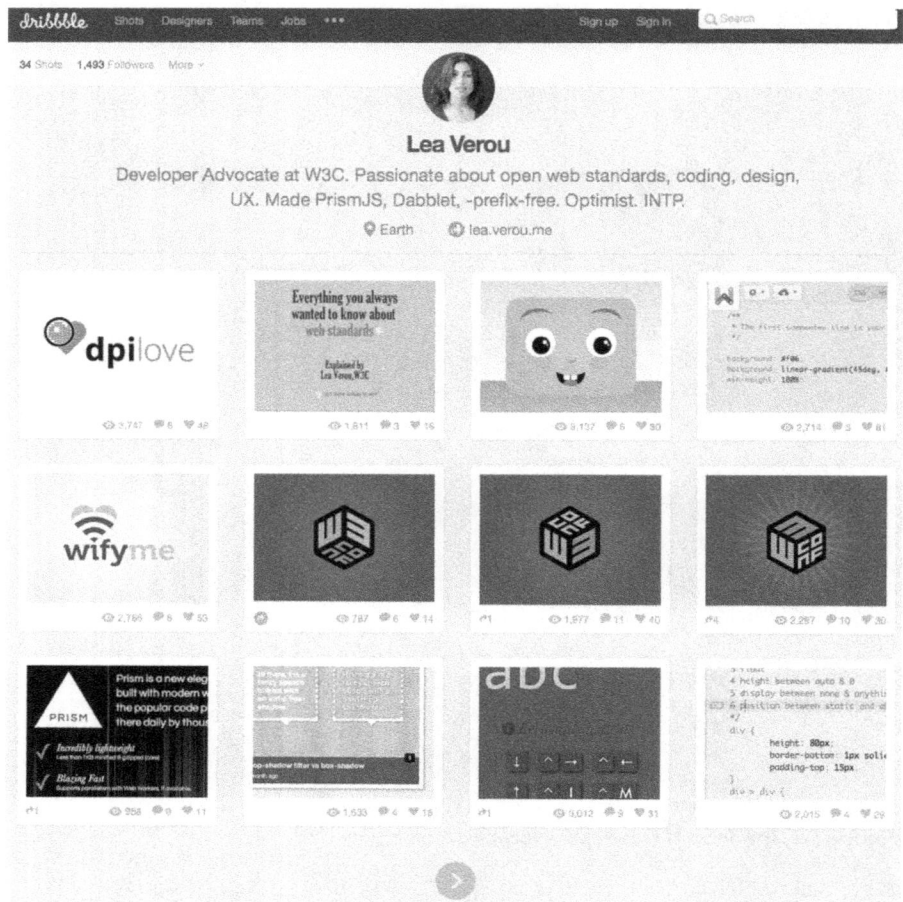

Figure 6-6. Lea Verou's Dribbble profile

Public Speaking Is for You, Too

I started this chapter with the most popular sites you can use to build your brand and show your expertise to the rest of the world. Now let's see what else you can do, and I'll start by the most popular one: public speaking. It's something many developers would like to do, and you may be one of these. Recently, I gave a train the trainer session in India, and when my colleague and I asked how many attendees would like to do public speaking, everyone in the room raised their hands. I totally understand this, because I like to do public speaking, and there are many good things associated with it. Here are some of them:

- Recognition by your peers and increased credibility
- Being seen as an expert from people outside of the industry
- The feeling of being a rock star on stage and in the conference materials

Of course, giving talks in public can help you on many levels, including gaining confidence and burnishing your technical skills, and it can definitely help your brand. I believe there is no better way to show others that you have a particular expertise than to share it in front of people.

There are many ways you can start speaking. Many conferences will give new speakers a chance. Identify the conference you would like to speak at (it will be easier to start with a local one) and follow them on their social media or website—most of them do a public call for speakers. That is the time to apply. Come up with an interesting abstract about a topic you know well that you would like to share with attendees. Your application may be rejected, because many conferences have way more suggestions than speaking slots available, but don't be discouraged.

You might try to find a camp event: unlike traditional conferences, the camp-style ones are generated by the attendees. They're usually less formal and give more chances to beginners. This is where I started as a public speaker. If you don't know where to start, check out sites like Lanyrd (http://lanyrd.com), an excellent repository for professional events, mostly conferences (see a search example with Python—http://lanyrd.com/search/?q=python). Not every conference uses Lanyrd, but it's quite popular.

Speaking at conferences: is what many developers want to do, but they're not the only places you can speak or start giving public talks. User groups are also quite popular. Most user group organizers are always looking for good content. I should know—I'm running one, and it's not always easy to find speakers when you have a monthly event. Because user groups usually meet every month or so, they're not as huge as conferences, but they're more open to new speakers, and it's less intimidating to speak there. Check out user groups near your hometown, with a focus on the technology you like, and contact the organizer.

Tip I suggest attending a user group at least once or twice before asking to speak. You want to see how it's working and talk to the organizer in person. You'll have a better impact by knowing the group and having this discussion face to face. Meetup (http://www.meetup.com) is an excellent site for finding local groups.

Chapter 6 | Weapons of Choice

As you can see in Figure 6-7, I searched for groups about HTML technology in Toronto, Canada. You'll see in the results that some groups are entirely dedicated to this technology, like HTML Toronto. Others don't focus only on HTML but have talks about other technology once in a while, like DevTO, another amazing group in Toronto.

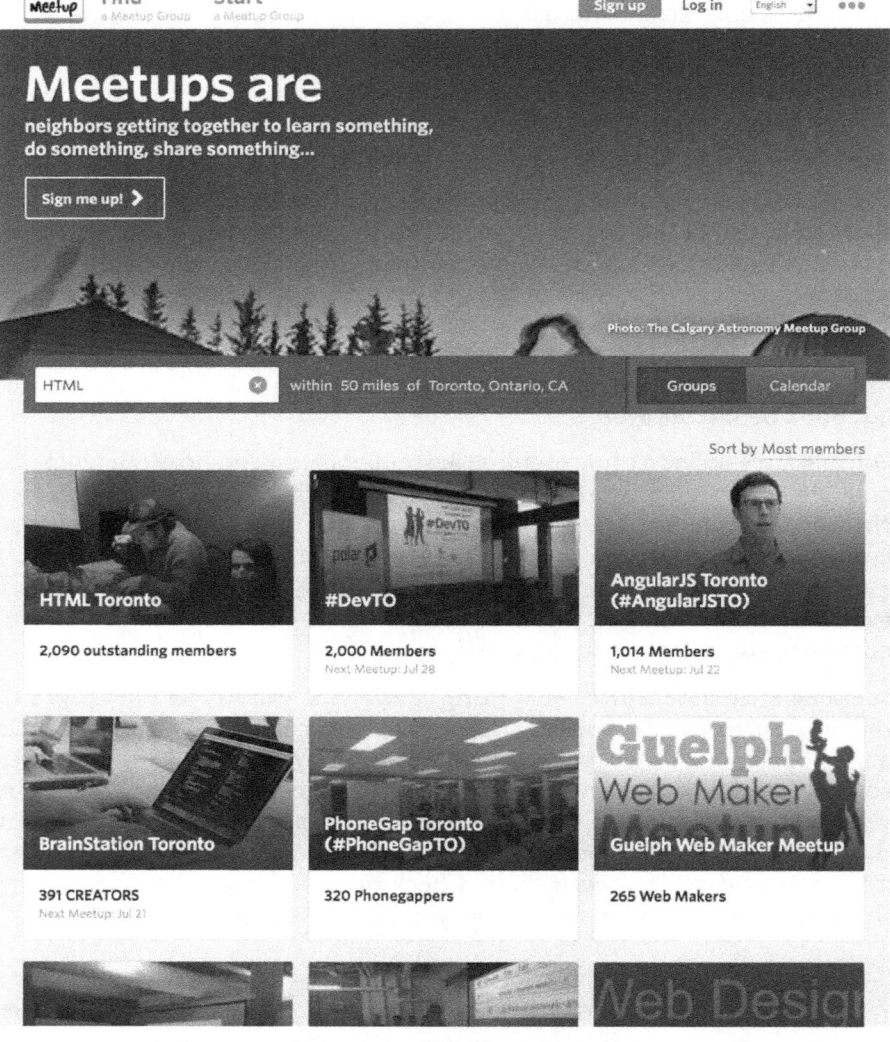

Figure 6-7. Looking for groups related to HTML in Toronto on Meetup.com

Some of those groups put on what they call *speaker idol* events. A little bit like the *American Idol* show, it's a special meetup where they open the mic to totally new speakers. In 15-minute talks, the new speakers do their presentations. In the end, they get feedback on their talk from industry experts who are used to speaking in front of a crowd. It's a good way to start speaking and get valuable feedback. It's not a common practice everywhere, but I know a few groups that have done this a couple of times in Montreal. "Idol" is a concept I would like to help spread a bit more. We used it in the train the trainer session in India, and it was a real success. A smaller presentation in a friendly environment with professional feedback is the perfect way to see if you really like doing it or not.

You may also want to start at your company or school. Maybe there's no existing group for such presentations right now, so why not create one? You can create a *lunch-and-learn* or *brown bag session*. As the name says, during lunch time, while your colleagues eat, you present to them about something. You could talk about a cool technology you just learned, one of the problems you solved at work, or the last technical book you read. No matter the topic, and no matter the amount of time you'll speak, the idea is to use lunch time to start talking. It can be intimidating to speak in front of friends and colleagues, but it's actually easier, because they will be friendlier (and, sure, may tease you gently) if something goes wrong.

Of course, there are public speaking clubs all over the world. The most well known is Toastmasters International (www.toastmasters.org). Joining a local Toastmasters club can be a good way to practice, find other speakers, and get great feedback.

What about your presentation itself? Let's see how you can extend it and scale it a bit more.

Sharing Your Slides

I've emphasized scaling your efforts in branding, and public speaking is no exception. You took the time to create great slides and deliver a fantastic talk. How can you reach more people than just the ones in the room? I've already told you how I do it: every time I finish a presentation, I upload the slides I used to SlideShare (http://www.slideshare.net). You can see my SlideShare profile (http://www.slideshare.net/fredericharper) in Figure 6-8.

Chapter 6 | Weapons of Choice

Figure 6-8. My SlideShare profile

Here again is a social concept with likes, followers, followings, and more. You can see which kinds of topics each member likes to share about. Your SlideShare profile is another way people can discover you online and find the information you have to share with them. However, because my slides are a visual support for my talk, and not the talk itself, they may or may not mean much to people who didn't attend the presentation. Nevertheless, it's an open door to my expertise. For example, people know by looking at my presentation on Responsive Web Design that I have the knowledge to be on stage.

As you can see in Figure 6-9, SlideShare helped me reach a lot more people than just giving presentations would. Sharing your slides becomes less about helping people learn about the topic and more about showing what you did, which is good for your brand. My last slide always shows a picture of me with my contact information (Figure 6-10). Obviously, my contact is there to help attendees reach me after my talk, but it also helps people who find my slides online know who I am and how to reach me. That could lead to a new speaking gig, book offers, new customers, and more. As for my picture, it's there to help people who saw my talk recognize me, but it's also for people who were not there, to know what I look like. (I use the same trick with my business card.)

Figure 6-9. Monthly email update from SlideShare

Figure 6-10. My usual last slide (again, with my face on it)

Recording Yourself

Another technique to reach more people with the talk you'll do is to record the talk and upload it somewhere. You don't need fancy equipment like an expensive camcorder (though the result would be better quality). I use software called Camtasia (www.techsmith.com/camtasia.html) from TechSmith, but many other packages can help you achieve the same goal. The idea is to record your screen, so people will have your slides, as well as your voice for the narration part. You can buy a fairly good inexpensive USB microphone, but I use the internal microphone of my computer. Even if the quality is not the best, it's good enough that people can listen to a one-hour talk without being annoyed.

After I record my talk, I do a minimum of editing (often just cutting in the beginning and the end) and then publish it on YouTube. By doing so, I get more eyeballs on my talk. It also gives people who were not there a chance to learn about the topic I shared at the event and enables the attendees to watch my talk again if they forgot something. As you can see in Figure 6-11, of the videos I uploaded to my YouTube profile have very low views, such as 15, but that's 15 more people I reached with my talk. One of my videos has attracted nearly a thousand views, so the small effort that it took me to press record and do a little editing is worth it. The number of views depends a lot on your brand, the conference promotion of your recording, the topic, the medium you use to publish it, how much of your network is on this medium, how people appreciate your presentation, and more.

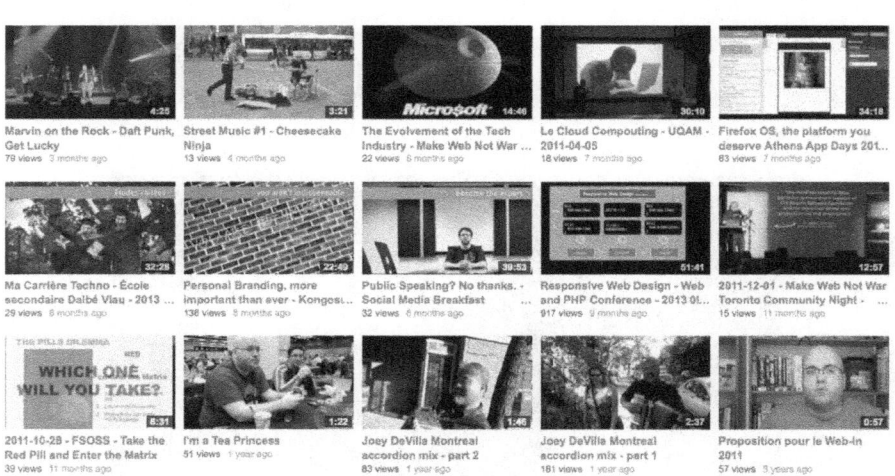

Figure 6-11. Some of the presentations I recorded (mixed with other videos I uploaded). Google and the Google logo are registered trademarks of Google Inc., used with permission

You Speak, You Blog

Back to your blog: you'll use it for a lot of things. You've uploaded your slides to SlideShare—or other service, like Speaker Deck (https://speakerdeck.com)—and uploaded your recording on YouTube (or other service, like Vimeo). Now you can write a blog post. It can take many forms, but blogging is a good way to get more valuable content and promote what you did by putting everything in the same place: your home on the web. Not everybody follows you on your other social media, and it's a good way to let Google know about what you did with some text (its preferred food).

Write a post about your experience at the event, about other talks, and also promote what you talked about. Embed the slides and videos and share the link to your post with friends and followers. I do this after every talk I give, so if someone asks me for material about my session, I only have to share one link, and it points to my site instead of other properties. I don't want my blog posts to be just about me but about helping conferences or other speakers get known. You can see an example of a post (http://outofcomfortzone.net/2014/04/28/fixing-the-mobile-web-with-firefox-os-at-fitc-toronto/) I did after my talk on Firefox OS at FITC Toronto in 2014.

Write a Book

It may seem like out-of-place advice from someone who is writing his first book, but writing a book is another great way to share your passion with others. On top of that, it's an amazing way to get visibility and credibility. As with everything else, if you don't try, you'll never succeed. So why not ask an editor (like someone at Apress) if they're interested in publishing your book about using Python and Pelican to generate static websites (or whatever your expertise is)? It may be as easy as that. Of course, not everyone can write or publish a book, but if it's been on your radar, you should go for it. I mentioned before that I got some offers, but for this book, it was a bit different. I wrote a blog post about the fact that I wanted to write a book on personal branding for developers, because it's one of my passions and I know many people who would benefit from managing and being conscious of their personal brand. Someone in my network saw my post and proposed to put me in contact with his editor at Apress. I sent an email, and a couple of days after, we worked out a contract for me to write this book!

Since then, when people hear that I'm writing a book, their perception changes about my expertise on personal branding. They ask me for advice, approach me for speaking gigs, and more. Writing a book (print or e-book) will help you share your expertise with a large audience and will help you achieve your goal in helping your brand grow.

Podcasts: Sharing without Writing

Not everybody is comfortable with writing, and most of the first section of this chapter is about writing. You need to go out of your comfort zone, and you'll get better by doing it often, but if it's not your thing, there are other ways to share your passion without having to write a lot. One way is to start a podcast. Podcasting is still a fabulous opportunity to share with others and gain visibility. It's easier than you think, and you don't need super-advanced equipment or extensive audio or video expertise to make it happen. You can do something good for cheap.

Audio Podcasting

Think of an audio podcast as an Internet radio show that people can listen to when they want. Perhaps you have an idea on a recurring theme you would like to share with others, like tips and tricks on C++. You could start with a monthly podcast of 30 to 60 minutes. To get good quality, you can buy a decent microphone for a little more than $100, and you're set to record amazing programs with good sound. You can start with your computer's built-in microphone. The sound quality will be lower, but again, you don't have to invest money to try it.

As for providing your masterpiece to the external world, it's not too complex. If you already have a blog and want to start an audio podcast, you can use a plugin like Blubrry PowerPress for Wordpress (http://create.blubrry.com/resources/powerpress/). I used it for my audio podcast, We Are Geek (a French-language podcast with an English name; now over). It's free, easy to use, and helps you maintain your podcast on services like iTunes. If you don't want to manage your podcast's site yourself, you can use services like PodBean (http://www.podbean.com), which have different price points but are mostly inexpensive for a small podcast with a low volume—perfect to start. At some point, you may want to upgrade your account to something better.

Video Podcasting

If you feel more inspired to do some videos (or you want people to see you), a video podcast is also a good idea. How about a series of interviews with other experts in your industry? That's what I started when I was at Microsoft: The Make Web Not War TV (http://outofcomfortzone.net/tag/make-web-not-war-tv/), which gave me the opportunity to interview people like Jonathan Snook and Josh Clark. Why did I interview other experts in the industry? The point is to help people know other experts. You'll regularly connect with your podcast audience as you release, say, a monthly video, and on top of that, you will connect with the experts you interviewed: a double win. In my case, I was on the same side of the camera, doing the interview, which is another way to get visibility. This is how I met people like Mike Kruzeniski, designer lead at Twitter, and Robert Giggey, the super-dedicated Open Data lead at the city of Ottawa.

How can you start? If the podcast is all about you talking to your audience, you could start by simply using your computer's build-in camera. If you want to share a demonstration on your computer, you can use screen recording software. If you take the interview path but can't or don't want to do them in person, you can use tools like Skype or Google Hangouts, which help you record remote discussions easily.

As for the rest, if you want better equipment, the money you spend can grow quickly, but it will always depend on how you want to spend it, how much quality you want, and your end goal. I started one of my projects, Portrait de blogueurs (http://outofcomfortzone.net/tag/portrait-de-blogueurs/), a video podcast which was a series of interviews with Montreal's bloggers, with an inexpensive video camera. The quality was good enough, but for the Make Web Not War TV project, I decided to level up the game and use my DSLR with wireless mic. The result was much better and a lot more professional.

Remember the section on volunteering in Chapter 5? There are many ways to give your time, and a good one is to become a mentor at hackathons and workshops. By doing so, you're using your expertise with the central technology of the workshop or one of the technologies used at the hackathon to help participants. You're not participating yourself (usually you don't have the time to do both), and your main goal is to support other developers who are not as savvy as you with the programming language they use. Often, mentors are featured on the event websites and by being one of the helpers, you'll be seen as an expert (and you are). It's a good way to help others, get credibility, show your skills, and create new contacts. You can use sites like Meetup or Lanyrd to find events where you can help. Trust me, the organizers will be more than happy to get your help, so don't be afraid to contact them, even if you don't know them personally.

Organize an Unconference, User Group, or Conference

To achieve big things, you need to think big. Why not start an unconference on big data in your city? If you want to keep the organization to a minimum, you could find a venue, put a wiki online, and promote it in your network. The speakers will practically line up for you. If you go camp style, the discussions will be built on site by the attendees. At the end of the day, no matter how much (or little) you participated in the conversations, or whether you spoke at the event, you are the creator.

It's a good thing to attend user groups, and it might be even better to create one. Many cities already have user groups, but even in those situations, there are still opportunities for more. Are a good number of developers working with technology X, but no monthly meetup is available? Start one! It's a bit more work to organize than an unconference (another word for camp), because you also need a venue for recurring meetings. It can be even more difficult to regularly find interesting speakers with interesting topics. Starting a user group is a tremendous opportunity to meet new people, get known in the community, and share your expertise: you're the organizer, and nothing stops you from giving the first talk in your newly formed group.

If there is interest about a particular technology, the group will grow organically if you have regular sessions. We started our HTML5mtl group three years ago, and we now have more than 1,000 members. Of course, that doesn't mean they all come to my monthly meetups, but it does mean a lot of people have an interest in HTML5. Because we started the group, everybody thinks we have expertise in it (because why would we have started the group if that were not the case?). It's powerful to start something, and so is the effect it produces. Quite often, it becomes how people perceive you.

People often see the project of starting a conference as something too big to tackle. Of course, it's a big time investment, and sometimes a big money investment, too, but it's something amazing to do. As an example, my friend Levin started Go Beyond Pixels and ran the conference for two years before putting his time into another project. I have no doubt that it was an amazing experience for him. If you get your hands dirty, find a good team to help you, and mobilize the community, you can do great things. Like everything else you'll do, the better it is, the bigger the impact it will have on your brand, so it's on you to start that new conference you always wanted to have in your city.

Professional Recognitions

When you want to show your expertise, you can display your experience and diplomas you earned at school—or you can go with more personal techniques, like the ones you just read about. There is another way, something I place between those two categories: professional recognitions.

Certifications are one of the most well-known means of recognition, and they are entirely based on your expertise with technology. Many companies and organizations, quite often through third-party companies like Prometric, offer certifications in their technologies. Many technologies offer certification tests you can take: Ruby, Java, Python, Microsoft technology, and more. You can also take certifications about a technique or role like ScrumMaster.

Of course, certifications will not replace experience entirely, and many people don't believe they're all that useful—but they can't hurt. In the worst case, the certification you have won't impress your next employer. But it may. I earned ScrumMaster at the Scrum Alliance when I was leading different projects, and MCSD (Microsoft Certified Solutions Developer) Programming in HTML5 with JavaScript and CSS3 when I was at Microsoft. The ScrumMaster helped me get back to work and lead a team of developers using the Scrum framework. They had confidence that even with no experience, I had the knowledge to lead a project using Scrum (reality is not always like in books or what you saw in class, but I had a good foundation). As for the HTML5 certification, it may or may not have helped me land my current job, but it certainly didn't hurt. In any case, think about your industry, and see whether a certification makes sense for you.

Certifications are earned by anyone who has enough knowledge to pass the exams or meet the requirements. Other recognitions from the industry are given to a few selected people. At Mozilla, we have what we call Mozilla Reps. As part of this program, some volunteers are recognized as official representatives of Mozilla. That means they are dedicated to our mission, have the knowledge, and have the passion for sharing with their local community. Not everybody gets this recognition. The MVP, a Microsoft recognition for Most Valuable Professional, is well perceived in the Microsoft ecosystem and has helped many people get better jobs, more contracts, and even speaking gigs.

Those are only two examples, but many more options are out there. Some have more value than others. Some are better known than others. Some have more impact in your area, industry, or expertise than another. In any case, like anything else in this book, see if certification makes sense for you, and make it one of your goals if you decide it can help you—but *only* if it can help you. Remember, it's nice to be recognized, but don't do it just for the trophy.

Be Consistent

As I've mentioned, try to use the same username where possible, use your real name everywhere, put up a picture of yourself.... Did you observe something in the previous pages? Did you see my face enough? As you can see, I used the same picture everywhere (except on my last slide, because the other one fit better). I try to update my picture once a year, and I also use the same username everywhere I can.

It's important to keep your biography on all sites accurate and up to date. I know it's not always easy: I tend to change them as I come across them (I should be more rigorous). Most of the time, it's no big deal. But think about when you change jobs. For a long time, my SlideShare profile said I was a technical evangelist at Microsoft while I was at Mozilla. That didn't give a good impression of how I'm managing my online presence. It could have caused some problems.

The idea here is to be consistent. Because I'm using my real name, and it's easy to recognize me on the pictures, every time you want to find information about me on different sites, you can just try to look for "Frédéric Harper" and you'll find it.

Remember   Be yourself, be visible, and be consistent: you want to be easily discoverable, so that what you've done will be, too.

Optimize *Everything*

So far, I've encouraged you to prioritize and learn to say no, but you still won't have time to do everything. You'll have to choose, and you'll have to optimize your workflow. I'll share some of my preferred tricks with you. This section talks about three important techniques I use every day to maximize my time, be more efficient, and concentrate on what I'm doing at the moment.

Trick 1: Keep Yourself Informed in an Optimized Way

Audiobooks are among my sources for learning about nontechnical things. I listen to books about self-improvement, efficiency, marketing, social media, and more. Most nonfiction books seem to be relevant to personal branding, whether or not the author knows it. Everything about social media, being a better developer, being more efficient, marketing, and so on can help you with your brand. (I've already mentioned some of the books that have inspired me, and I'll give you more suggestions in the last chapter.)

I know some people prefer physical, old-school, paper books. I personally don't care, as my relation is not with the book itself but what it contains. I don't mind listening to a book instead of reading one on paper or on a screen. It's not about being lazy or not being able to read. Audiobooks give you the opportunity to "read" in situations where it would be difficult to do so: walking, for example, or driving. In fact, whenever you listen to music, such as while commuting, you could be listening to a book. When I go to the gym for an hour, I listen to a book. In other words, I maximize my time by doing two things at once.

I personally use Audible (www.audible.com) from Amazon. I've been a member for almost a year now, and I've listened to 13 books—12 more than last year! The plan I have is a small one: for about $15 a month, I get one credit, and that gives me the opportunity to buy a book. I can listen to those on iTunes on my computer, in any Audible application, or even with the music application on phones.

Another way to get information is through good blogs and websites using an RSS (Really Simple Syndication) feed. By using an RSS client, I can have all my information in one place. I don't have to open all the websites and find the new information myself: the client does the job for me—I just have to read the content I receive. If you try RSS, keep in mind that you need to curate your sites list often to update them, and be sure you always have the best sources of information out there. That doesn't mean you can't read elsewhere—you need different opinions from the ones you're used to—but RSS can save you a lot of time. The client downloads content for offline reading, so even on the subway or the plane, you can read your news and blog posts without an internet connection.

There are many RSS clients out there. I use the free version of a feed aggregator called Feedly (http://feedly.com). Feedly's job is to update the list of articles you have to read by syncing with the RSS feeds you are subscribed to regularly. I prefer to use the client on my computer, even when there is an online version available: it's more convenient, and I need to be able to read without Internet access.

One of the clients I use on my phone is Newsify (http://newsify.co) (Figure 6-12). One of its main features is that it syncs with your Feedly account. In other words, it is not syncing with all the RSS, but just with the Feedly server. Feel free to look in the marketplace of your preferred device: you'll find many RSS clients, and a lot of them are free, even without ads.

Chapter 6 | Weapons of Choice

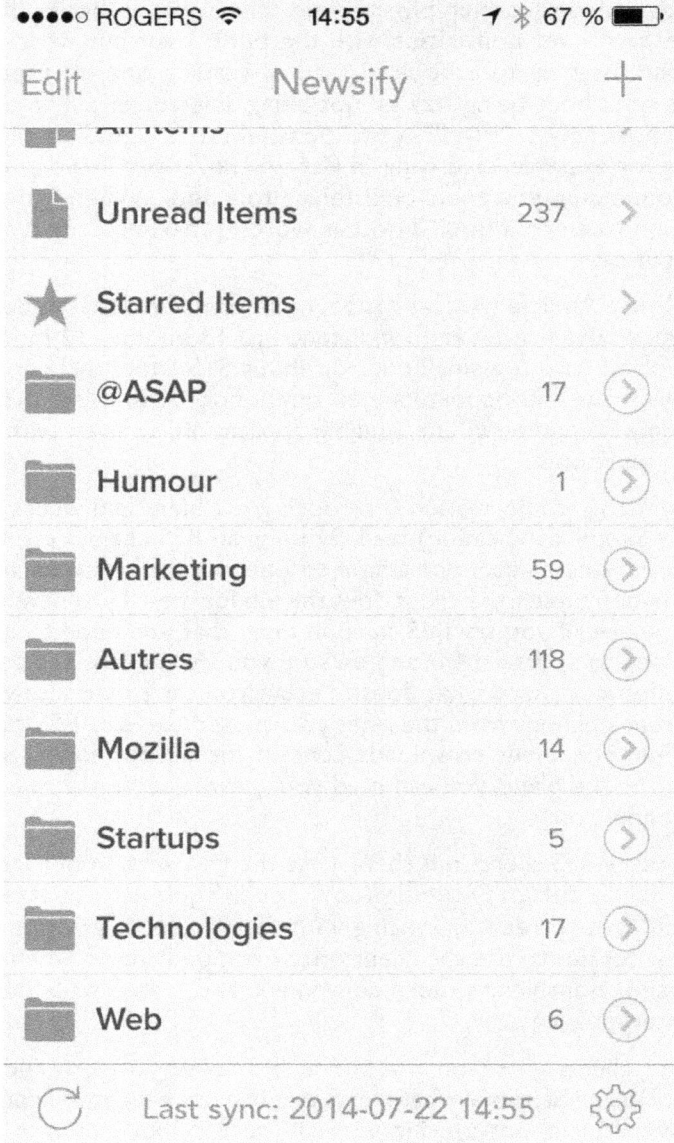

Figure 6-12. Newsify, an iOS RSS reader that connects to Feedly

On OS X, I use an application called ReadKit (http://readkitapp.com). ReadKit does the same thing Newsify does on OS X: syncs with my Feedly account and gives me offline support, including images in articles. On top of that, it connects with my Pocket (http://getpocket.com) account, which brings me to the last tool I'm using for this first trick.

Success in Programming

What do you do when you find an interesting link that someone shares on Twitter or sends you on email, but you don't have the time to read the article right then? Instead of adding to your browser tabs of death (an expression I just invented), you can add the article to read later in your Pocket account (Firefox and Chrome plugins available). In the end, it gives you a view like your RSS reader. The iOS app works great, with offline support. On OS X, ReadKit is doing the job. Of course, as you can see in Figure 6-13, I'm way behind with my reading list, but at least they're all in the same place, and I can read them as soon as I have the time—or should I say, when I take the time to prioritize them.

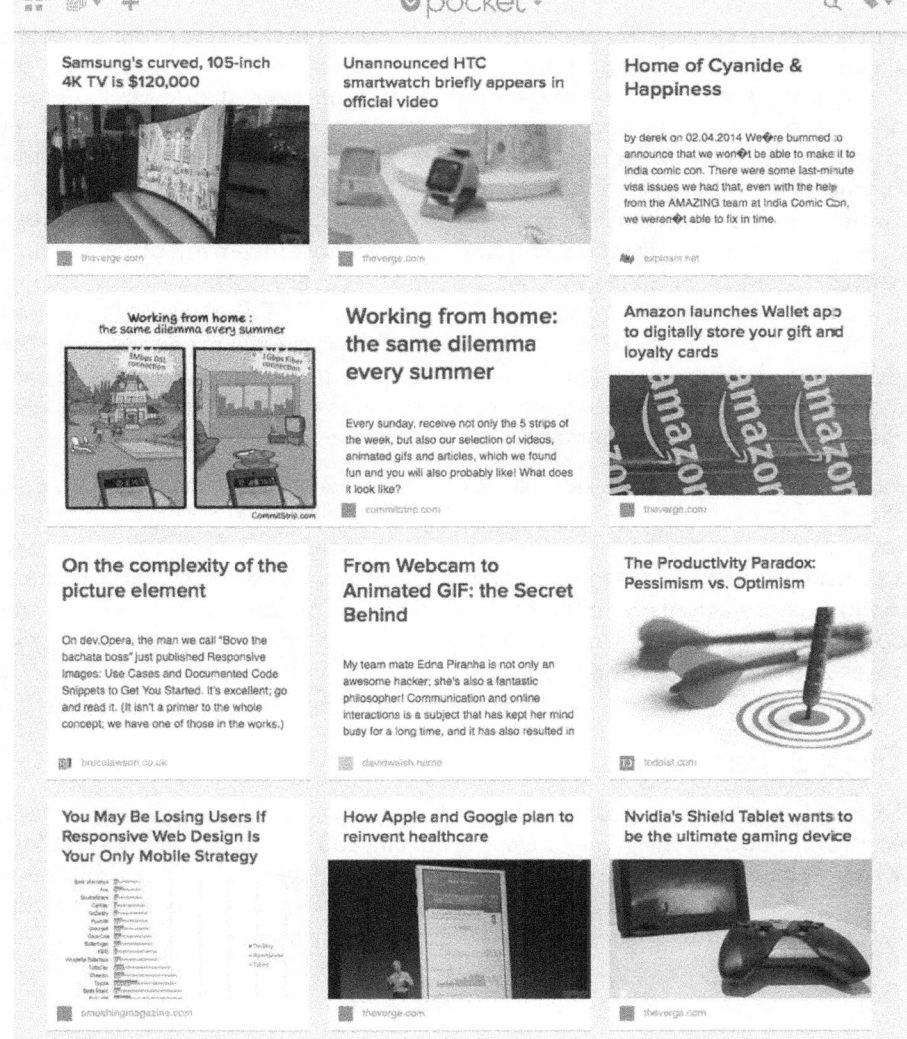

Figure 6-13. Some unread articles on my Pocket account

To sum up, I have many sources of information (probably too many) but I can find them all in three places: audiobooks, Feedly, and Pocket. It's easier for me to find, read, or listen to them: no time lost!

Trick 2: Don't Trust Your Memory

If there's one thing I've learned, it's that I cannot trust my memory. No relation to my age (hey, I'm still young!) or my abilities: we just cannot trust our memories. There are so many things happening in a day, and so many things you're thinking about, that there is a good chance you'll forget something.

It may seem annoying to some people, but I take notes for everything—useful articles I read, some quotes from a book, notes from a meeting, ideas for a blog post, suggestions I want to give to my manager at our next one-on-one meeting. Anything and everything goes into multiple notes in one of my digital notebooks on Evernote (http://evernote.com/). If you don't know Evernote, the tagline says it all: *Remember Everything*. I even use my digital notebook for personal stuff like recipes, notes of games I loan to friends, and more. I can connect it my digital notebook (I use Evernote) to many other services because there is an online API. As an example, every time I tweet, a backup is made in one of my Evernote notebooks using IFTTT (http://ifttt.com). Because the search engine on Twitter doesn't always fulfill my needs, Evernote gives me an easier way to search my own tweets. It's also a way for me to back them up, in case anything happens to my social media accounts. I do this with Facebook statuses and Foursquare check-ins, too.

Because Evernote is quite popular, it's also connected with many other applications. For example, in Newsify, if I found an article interesting, I can send it to Evernote directly so I can use some references for a future blog post or a presentation. By putting everything in Evernote, it's easier to find the information. There are many other tools on different platforms that give you this opportunity, so find the one that makes sense for you. No matter what, take notes and don't trust your memory.

Trick 3: Focus

To focus, you need a clear mind. That's why I use a suggestion from David Allen in his book *Getting Things Done* (Penguin, 2002): every time I have an idea for something I need to do, I add it to my task manager if I can't do it immediately. That way I won't forget to send that bug report to my colleague or that I absolutely need to clean the air conditioner filter before summer.

There's also a pleasant side effect of saving this task somewhere: you'll be able to remove it from your head. Let's say your spouse told you not to forget to buy a pint of milk before you left home this morning. During the day, once in a while, you'll think about that request because you didn't buy the milk yet. By committing this task to paper or in the digital task manager (or calendar) with an alarm, you can forget it. Your application will remember for you. It's good for tasks that are not important, too: you may not set an alarm, so you may not remember to do that task during the day, but one moment, when you check your task management system, you'll see that task and will do it.

There are dozens of popular task management systems. You can use paper if you prefer, like a cool Moleskine notebook. The idea is to empty your mind so you can focus on the task you have to do at this exact moment. Right now, I'm using Doit.im (http://doit.im).

I have attention deficit issues (seriously, my doctor told me). I'm dealing with it well without medication. I can't focus for too long on a task, so I use something called the Pomodoro Technique (http://pomodorotechnique.com). I focus on one task for 25 minutes and then take a 5-minute break. I achieve a lot more by doing this and splitting my tasks into chunks of work. It may be a good way of working for you, even more if you tend to be distracted by other things like social media (whether or not you have ADHD). There's a free book by the technique's inventor if you want to read more about the topic. Many other techniques exist to help you focus at work, get more done, and be more efficient. Find the one that makes you do awesome things!

There are many other ways to optimize your time, such as working at home (you may want to ask your manager or find a job that gives you this opportunity). In any case, the idea is to maximize the impact you'll have with the time you have, and there is no better way to start than by being more efficient.

Is Your Toolbox Full?

In this chapter, you learned about blogging, guest blogging, commenting in the blogosphere, participating in open source, helping at hackathons and workshops, starting to do public speaking, writing a book, doing podcasts, and targeting some industry recognition. You gained some knowledge about tools like GitHub, bug trackers like Bugzilla, StackOverflow, wikis like MDN, Dribbble, Meetup, Lanyrd, and SlideShare.

Do you have enough weapons to choose from? Did you choose which one to focus on first? Do you have an idea which technique will be beneficial for your own personal brand? Do you know any other tools I didn't include? (Let me know, and it may make it into future editions of this book.)

Chapter 6 | Weapons of Choice

We have a nearly infinite number of tools, services, sites, and techniques we can use to work on our brand, make it known, get expertise visibility, and reach our goals. This chapter focuses on the ones the industry knows most, and not without good reason: they're also the ones that yield the greatest impact. The tools covered here are the ones that will help you build your brand by gaining credibility, reaching more people, and showing your expertise to the rest of the world. Choose wisely!

CHAPTER 7

The Secret Ingredient: Your Tribe

Your Network Is Your Most Important Tool

> *It is better to be alone than in bad company.*
>
> —George Washington

You'll see in this chapter how people you know online will be critical to your success. The interview here is with someone I've never met in person. We follow each other, talk on Twitter once in a while, and once even worked for the same company. Rey Bango is principal software development engineer at Microsoft. He is well respected in the industry, and not too long ago, he was leading the evangelists team at Telerik.

Let's see if Rey thinks personal branding is important for developers.

> *I think for a developer, a more important factor is thought leadership and genuineness. Those two areas determine whether your message will be relevant to the community you're trying to engage with. The genuineness helps to reinforce your thought leadership if people feel they can get honest and thoughtful feedback from you on a specific topic. To me, that's way more important than building a personal brand and allows you to build deeper and more meaningful relationships.*

I get Rey's point, but I don't think one prevents the other. As you read in previous chapters, to be successful with your brand, it's critical to be genuine: you need to be true to yourself. *Leadership* is a term that appears quite often when people talk about a personal brand: often, you will find that leaders have visible, strong brands.

If you keep in mind the thoughts from different leaders and developers who shared their insights so far in this book, one thing will stand out: speaking loud and clear about personal branding is not common. People prefer to be humble, use different words for it, and even avoid the question entirely. Be proud of your brand! There is nothing wrong with being conscious of it and wanting to reach the next level.

Did personal branding help Bango to reach where he is right now, doing what he loves for a living? The answer may surprise you.

> *It really didn't. I don't think in terms of the "Rey Bango" brand. I prefer to focus on helping the community, promoting what's good for developers, and being genuine. And I think that's resonated with many developers who in many cases see me as an involved community member who truly wants to help.*

It's important to be conscious of your brand; anybody who knows Rey will tell you he has a strong one. He does a lot for the community, which has helped his brand include 'involved community member who truly wants to help." He is one of the founders of the jQuery Project. Who among web developers has never used jQuery or doesn't know about it? Rey's goal was to give to the community and probably create a framework he needed and would like to use. It's what he was doing as an evangelist and a developer, promoting what was good for his peers. Taking all this in consideration, that is the kind of thing that helped Rey be where he is now: well recognized and loved by the IT community.

■ **Remember** Don't work on your brand simply for the sake of working on your brand. Everything you do for others, your employer, and your community will have an impact on your brand as your end goal. Without being selfish, there is nothing wrong with thinking about yourself and your needs.

Rey also has good advice for us:

> *Stay humble, listen, and speak with everyone. Notice I used the word "with" there. That was purposeful. It's important to have two-way conversations, not just speak at people. Developers want to share their thoughts, and it's important to lend an ear to every developer since each one has a unique and interesting story to tell. I see too many of my peers wrapped up in*

themselves or in their cool-kid cliques and don't take the time to have conversations with broad audiences. I made that mistake myself early on in my career and thankfully I learned from it. And if you can be a mentor, it will pay dividends in the future both personally and professionally.

According to Rey, it's all about working, listening, speaking, and sharing with others. I can't agree more, and I'm glad to know such a wise man.[1] You can follow him on Twitter (https://twitter.com/reybango).

In Seth Godin's book *Tribes: We Need You to Lead Us* (Portfolio Hardcover, 2008), he defines a *tribe* as any group of people, large or small, who are connected to one another, a leader, and an idea. The idea of having a tribe is powerful. I think it's the secret ingredient missing to achieving your end goals and being successful with your personal brand. Your network, after all, is what will help you reach the next level. No network, no tribe, no audience—and that means no brand.

It's All About Your Network

What would happen if you worked on your brand and did amazing things, but only shared them with an empty room? How would you have any impact in this world? It's a lot harder to scale when you have no audience. Giving a speech in front of a mirror has little effect (except if you need to motivate yourself). To be successful, you need to have a tribe, a community. People who will love you, people who will argue with you, people that know you, people you know, friends, family, co-workers, mentors, mentees, inspirations, and so on. To have an impact, you need to build that tribe, you need to have someone to talk to. You need to get some visibility.

I'm not talking about a company culture where you need to send those victory emails to be noticed and successful. You should never have to do that, because your actions should speak for themselves. I'm talking about your tribe, that network of people you respect and who respect you, the people who will be there to help you and who you help. I can't use the word *network* too much. In today's world, knowing the right people and being known by the right people is one of the keys to success. You won't succeed without talent or expertise just because you know someone, but your network is an undeniable asset and is in fact crucial for your success.

I might not have the job I have today were it not for my network. When I decided to leave my previous job, I wrote a blog post to announce that I was looking for a new challenge. My network did an amazing job. People were sharing my post on Twitter, Facebook, LinkedIn, Google+, at work, with friends, and so on. It was and still is the most popular post on my site in terms of number of views. My network helped me have great discussions with potential employers, and I got good job offers. I had the pleasure of choosing where I wanted to work next. It's an opportunity not everybody has, but because of my network (as part of my brand), I had this privilege. The team I joined had three technical evangelist positions and had already filled two of them when I learned about the opportunity. They had many good applicants, but because I knew people on the team, my résumé was taken more seriously, even if the manager did not know me. Of course, they didn't hire me just because I knew people on the team, but because I had the skills and experience they were looking for. I was interviewed quickly because someone put my résumé on top of the pile. Skills, experience, and talent are necessary—but often only your network will help you get a chance to use these.

Who Is Your Tribe?

You can't please everyone, and some people are *not* your target audience. (Politicians understand this. Even if their goal is to make the masses love them, they focus on where they have the most chance to get votes or the best chances of swaying undecided voters.) That means you can't make everybody part of your tribe. You can't talk to everybody. You will have to choose who your audience is and focus on those people. Doing so also helps you choose the tools to put your energy in.

How do you choose your tribe? You can imagine a persona. You can create the ideal profile, a picture in time of one person who would be the ideal member of your tribe, the person you know would be receptive to your message. Let's start with my ideal tribe persona as an example for my technical evangelist job at Mozilla, an undeniable part of my brand:

> *A developer between 20 and 50 years old, whose day job is to build applications using web technologies like HTML, CSS, and JavaScript. He understands English even if it's not his primary language, and can live everywhere in the world. He is excited about new technology and believes enough in the open web as a platform to try a new operating system.*

If you read this description carefully, you will understand who my target audience is: a developer who creates web applications using HTML and has chances to port his application to Firefox OS (hence the "try a new operating system"). That does not mean that I can't talk to other type of developers; this persona is what you might call the low-hanging fruit. It's the kind of person easier for me to reach, connect with, and bring my branding forward. This kind of person is the first to add to my tribe, to build momentum, and to have an audience.

Now it's your turn to define your tribe member persona. Look at your brand statement from Chapter 6. Be as explicit as you can. The more specific you are, the better return on investment you will get. Start brainstorming by writing a bunch of words that would be related to that perfect fictitious person in your tribe. You can use those criteria to start working on your persona:

1. Where do they live?
2. What job are they doing?
3. What are their hobbies?
4. Do they have a special expertise?
5. What are their goals in life?
6. What do they like?
7. What don't they like?
8. How do they connect with you?
9. Which programming language(s) do they use?
10. Where do they go (websites, conferences, social medias, user groups, etc.)?

These are just some example questions you can ask yourself to help you create that persona. Sometimes, as with my own persona, it's not possible to be more precise: my target audience is very much my actual job, and this may be the case for you, too.

Write a short paragraph about this ideal person. The goal is to be able to read that paragraph to someone else, who will easily be able to picture the persona. They may even be able to think about people in their network who fit the bill.

Read it out loud to yourself (unless you are in a public area). How does it sound? Is there a way for you to focus on that audience? I'm sure there is, and it's your starting point. There is nothing to stop you (as with everything else in this book) from modifying and changing your description of that persona the more you move forward with your brand. You will need to adapt and change the criteria to adjust to new realities as they develop.

Go Where They Go

Now that you've created that picture of the perfect person to be your perfect audience, it's time to focus on it. Where do they hang out, offline and online? What tools do they use? What are the best ways to reach them? You will have to do your homework and find answers to these questions.

Pay attention to the tools, the events, and the sites your audience focuses on. In other words, go where they go. As an example, StackOverflow is an amazing tool, but it make no sense to burn precious time there if no one from your tribe—no one from your target audience—goes there. It's the same for every tool mentioned in the last chapter. Keep this in mind when you think about your tribe and where to put your effort and time. In the end, time is money, and we are not all rich.

The Not-So-Virtual World

Knowing people online is important. There are people you will never meet in person but with whom you can have an online relationship, like the one I have with Rey Bango. There are also people you meet online—on Twitter, Facebook, LinkedIn, the blogosphere, or elsewhere—who will become friends, business partners, customers, or acquaintances in real life, not just behind a screen.

Some of my best friends are people I met online. Some became partners in different projects—the kind of projects that help your brand if they're well targeted, even if they are only meant to give back to the community. A good example is my friend and colleague Debbie Rouleau. We first followed each other on Twitter. At one point, we met at a social event in Montreal. Since then, I've called her a friend. She took an active part in some projects I started. She has been one of my working partners on many occasions. She was part of the managing team for GeekFest Montreal (part of the core geek team, leading other volunteers), and she co-hosted an audio podcast with me. And it all started with a tweet I made for a conference I was attending.

The first contract I got was from Jacques Plante from Radio Highway, a French radio show for truck drivers, via Twitter. He knew me online, heard that I was starting as a freelancer, and had a good impression of my professionalism. I had never met him or the man who had put us in contact.

Don't underestimate the power of online relationships. You never know where they will take you, and even if I prefer offline relations (more on that later), I value those made online.

Amplify Online

A recurring theme on this book is scaling. There is no better way to scale than by using your online channels and network. You started to build that network by creating a blogbut that is not the only channel you have. You were using SlideShare to build a new audience and scale the last presentation you did. On top of that, you published a recording of the video you did on YouTube or Vimeo. Those are all good things to do, but you can do more!

Let's see how some of the most popular social media sites can help you amplify and scale what you have to share. I won't write about all the services available, because there are too many, but I selected the ones that, based on my experience, I think will help you the most.

Twitter

After my blog, Twitter is my preferred social media, but this is not the case for everyone. Many people use Twitter only to post pictures of their cat or food or to gripe about the weather. (I'm guilty of those things as well.) Even so, Twitter is a great asset to build an audience.

I love sharing my thoughts in 140 characters. It helps maximize impact and, most important, clear my thoughts. But that's not the only advantage. It's easy to build a network on Twitter, because it takes little commitment from either side. There is no mutual engagement on Twitter: I can follow you even if you are not following me and vice versa. It does not involve the strong word *friend*, like Facebook does. Following and followed, it's that simple. Of course, not everybody uses Twitter, but there is a chance that a good chunk of the population related to your persona uses it. At every conference I go to, pretty much everyone in the room has a Twitter account, so it's quite popular in the IT world.

I use Twitter on a personal and professional basis. My contact information on my slides and on business cards contains my email address, website, and my Twitter ID (@fharper). I tweet about everything. More important, I use Twitter to amplify everything else I do. Remember the scaling flow of my presentation: I do my presentation, post the slides on SlideShare, post the recording on YouTube, and do a blog post including everything available. It doesn't stop there. After that, I tweet my post online. Why should you do this, too? After all, you have a blog, and people can subscribe to your RSS feed, or your email update. It's simple: many people won't subscribe to your blog, but will still want some update on interesting topics once in a while, and Twitter is a good place to find interesting things to read.

Tip Despite the ephemeral nature of tweets, Twitter is the biggest source of readers for my blog after search engines.

Facebook, Google+, and the Like

I'm not a huge fan of Facebook, but it's not easy to live in today's world without a Facebook account. I use it to amplify what I do elsewhere, like sharing a blog post. My network on Facebook is not all technical people, and it still drives some readers to me. You can start a Facebook group with people with the same interests, like a group for people using R in Prague. By starting a group, your leadership becomes evident, and you can get an impressive troupe of people to add to your personal network. You could start a page for fans of different technologies. The tools are there! All you have to do is use them.

Facebook is the most popular social media out there, but consider using Google+, Pinterest, Tumblr, and others you might not think would be useful, like Instagram, Yelp, or even Foursquare. I use Instagram on a personal level, but it's still beneficial for my brand, because I post pictures once in a while from events I participate in or other geeky stuff.

In general, it's important to show a human side: you are not just about your expertise in computing-related stuff. Some friends of mine make a clear distinction between their personal and professional lives, but I blur the line a little more. (Maybe such a distinction is harder with my kind of job.) Some people connect with me on Instagram, and by doing so end up connecting with me at another level, like LinkedIn. I use Instagram to cross-post pictures automatically to my Twitter and Facebook accounts, providing those followers and friends with other great content. Some social media experts will tell you not to do this, but remember: the best way to use social media is the way that works for you.

Social Media Can Be for Technical People, Too

A few ears ago, the Slashdot (http://slashdot.org) effect referred to the impact a huge site (like Slashdot) caused when it linked to a smaller site. Quite often, the small site was not prepared for that kind of traffic and slowed down, became unresponsive, and even went down due to the unusually high number of people visiting it. Many websites are similar to Slashdot. One of them is Hacker News (https://news.ycombinator.com) (see Figure 7-1).

Figure 7-1. The Hacker News front page

As you can see, there is nothing special about the design of Hacker News, but it's a very popular news aggregator for a technical audience. The voting system helps readers find relevant content and represents an opportunity for you. Every time you create a post that could interest this community, making an entry here is a way to promote it. I do this with my technical blog posts, and we do this with our posts on the Hacks blog at Mozilla. It's a way to reach more people interested in technical topics. Don't expect to get *slashdotted* (hit by a storm of readers) right away, and maybe it will never happen, but you will likely gain some viewers. Bear in mind that a community like Hacker News can be tough. They may not be as friendly as your co-worker on your latest blog post, but that's part of the joy of publishing your ideas and projects on the Internet.

As far as developers trying to gain credibility and work on their personal brand, let me share another trick with you. Remember Lanyrd? It's an amazing site to get information on events near you or conferences where you would like to present—and it's also a great way to share your speaking experience with the rest of the world. Once you have a public profile, people can see what you've done, and you may get a new speaking gig by showing where you spoke before.

Of course, there are other ways to do this. I have my own speaking page (http://outofcomfortzone.net/speaking/) on my site, as you can see on Figure 7-2. I maintain control over my data and how it's displayed, and I don't have to fear that tomorrow Lanyrd will close, cancel my account, or be replaced by something else. On the other hand, it has less impact, because now people have to go on my site to see where I spoke. It can work all right when give a link for a speaker application I'm doing, but there is less of a chance that people will find me and offer me a speaking role. That's why I'll probably move my speaking experience to Lanyrd, copying the way Robert does it: adding myself to some events, creating ones not listed, and so on. As I've said, there is nothing wrong with copying smart moves by others, as long as you're not copying everything.

You can also share bits of code, and not just full projects, by using a site like Snipplr (http://snipplr.com) or by creating Gist (https://gist.github.com) on GitHub. On Snipplr, you even have a reputation system, as with StackOverflow (though not as complex).

Success in Programming

SPEAKING EXPERIENCE

This is an exhaustive list of all the speaking I did: keynotes, presentations, and panels. You can find the slides, the video recording, and even recap blog posts (details label) for some of them.

P.S.: Keep in mind that even if many talks have the same title, it's always a different talk as my content is always updated, adapted to the crowd, and delivered in a different way.

UPCOMING (5 EVENTS)

22 Oct 2014	**HTML FOR THE MOBILE WEB, FIREFOX OS** *(TALK)* **ALL THINGS OPEN** Reigh, United States
31 Oct 2014	**OPEN OPERATING SYSTEMS AND MOZILLA'S VISION ON THE FUTURE** *(TALK)* **TELEFONICA MOVE** Montevideo, Uruguay
7 Nov 2014	**HTML POUR LE WEB MOBILE, FIREFOX OS** *(TALK)* **DEVFEST NANTES** Nantes, France
18 Nov 2014	**BEGINNERS GUIDE FOR BUILDING A PERSONAL BRANDING IN THE DEVELOPER COMMUNITY** *(TALK)* **CODEMENTOR OFFICE HOURS** Online conference
24 Nov 2014	**OPENSOURCE BUSINESS MODELS EVENT** *(PANEL)* **HEC MONTRÉAL** Montréal, Canada

PAST (106 EVENTS)

Figure 7-2. My speaking page on my blog, listing where I've spoken

LinkedIn: The Résumé Is Dead, Long Live the Résumé

Maybe GitHub is the new résumé for developers, but as I've already mentioned, I don't think this is entirely accurate. On the other hand, I firmly think that the paper version of a curriculum vitae is dead. I haven't used one since my first job. I'm always surprised when companies or headhunters ask me for a Word document or a paper copy of my résumé. I personally think LinkedIn is the new king—I've used my LinkedIn profile (http://ca.linkedin.com/in/fredericharper) as my résumé for years now. If headhunters really want a document, I send them a PDF of my profile. (By the way, feel free to add me as a connection!) You may even reach a point where people won't care about your LinkedIn profile—your actions and personal brand will speak for themselves.

LinkedIn is a résumé on steroids. Of course, you have your work experience, but if you do a good job completing your profile, it will be an exhaustive list of your achievements and experiences and a powerful tool to showcase your expertise and your brand. Here are the kinds of things I list on my profile

1. **Summary:** Think about your elevator pitch. This is a good place to add some catchy sentences about who you are, what you do/did, and what you are looking for.

2. **Skills & Endorsements:** I consider this section to be a bit like a popularity contest, but many people think it's important. These can be based on your experience, or based on the fact that people *think* you have that expertise, you can clearly see a pattern (in my case, you can see on the top of the list skills like HTML5, Web development, JavaScript, blogging, public speaking).

3. **Experience:** I decided to list only *jobs* I have had in this section—no special projects, except one experience I named *Public speaker, blogger, and doer* for outofcomfortzone.net, because I wanted people to see that it's an integral part of my experience. It's important that people who view my profile know that I do public speaking and like it. It's also important to me that they know I blog and I'm a doer.

4. **Publications:** This is where I list any significant contributions in magazines or online publications (this book is already listed). It's an occasion to say that I contributed to other properties, not just my own. You can write for magazines or online publications in addition to your and others' blogs.

5. **Projects:** This is a list of projects I've worked on. I decided to list only applications I created. This isn't a big priority on my profile, because I don't consider any of those to give a big "wow" effect, but I'm still proud of them. I prefer to show everything else first, because that works better for the type of jobs I'm doing now and probably in the future.

6. **Volunteer Experience & Causes:** This section is very important for me, because it's where I list the volunteering I've done and projects I've created or participated in (GeekFestMtl, FailCamp Montreal, HTML5mtl, YulDev, etc.). They are critical to my brand, the foundation of who I am: a doer. I could have put them at the top of my profile, but as amazing as I think those things are (yes, it's important to be proud of what you've achieved), these aren't the first things people look for in a résumé—and keep in mind that LinkedIn is an online CV.

7. **Honors & Awards:** Here I listed my MVP (Microsoft Most Valuable Professional) nomination regarding HTML5. This is a good section to brag about those kinds of things.

8. **Certifications:** This section's position may depend on how you perceive the certifications you have or how your industry sees them. I'm proud of the two I've earned, but they are not as important to me as everything else before in this list. Not everything can be first on the list—you have to prioritize according to impact.

9. **Education:** My skills and experience are the most important things I want people to know about me. It's a good section to list your diplomas and degrees. Feel free to move it to the top of the list if there is more value to you. If you just got out of school, this section should definitely be at the top, as you don't have as much experience.

10. **Organizations:** Here is where you can show what groups you're a member of. It's a great way to show your interests to the rest of the world. You can even duplicate some organizations: it's what I did with the W3Québec. I have been a member for a couple of years, but I was also on the board of directors for one mandate. It's a great section to showcase the volunteering you've done as a way to connect with others.

11. **Languages & Additional Info:** Depending of the type of the job you have, the languages section may be important. As an example, you may land a specific type of job if you speak Spanish. If you want to move to another country, you may need to show your languages skills on top of the list. Like all the elements in a profile, what you list here is subjective and related to your goal. My profile is in English, and for me, that's important: people will understand that I know this language from my profile (I decided not to duplicate my profile in French, an excellent feature of LinkedIn). I use the additional information section to specify how and why you should contact me.

You can also add sections on test scores, courses, and patents. All in all, LinkedIn gives a nearly complete view of your experience and what you can do for a customer or future employer. There is no other place, not even my blog, where you can so easily see the big picture of my professional life. The idea is to maximize the impact you want to have, so make your LinkedIn profile truly yours. It's an amazing tool that has been useful in many parts of my life.

LinkedIn also has another huge advantage: it's a social media platform, not just a web version of your past experiences that used to be on paper. The Recommendations section is a big part of this. More often than not, it's an exchange of "write me a recommendation, and I will write you one," but even so, it's interesting for future clients or employers to see how other professionals view you in their own words.

For me, the most amazing feature on LinkedIn is the potential for professional connections. It's an amazing way to connect with previous coworkers, current colleagues, clients, and other people in your industry. Some people only add connections they've had a professional experience with (it's how LinkedIn is designed), but others will add anyone who requests a connection. Having a great network on LinkedIn is really powerful, as it gives a view of your network to others, and as you learn later, that can be helpful. Having those connections available also gives you the opportunity to help your contacts get in touch with other people in your network, which you should do as often as you can. This large network also helps you find people who can help you at some point. For example, many headhunters use LinkedIn to recruit new talent, and you can get some interesting offers.

If you don't have a LinkedIn profile, create one right now. It's not negotiable. You need to be there, even if you are not looking for a job. In fact, the best time to do it is when you already have a job, because that way when you really need it, it will already be there, ready to work for you.

In Your Face

There is nothing like meeting or knowing someone in person. Online relationships are necessary, but they are still mostly relations with strangers—people you don't really know. When you meet someone in person, your relationship reaches a new level. You know each other a little bit, no matter how short the meeting or the discussion was. No matter how seldom you interact with that person on a personal or professional basis, you know each other face to face.

For most people, that changes something. Many people don't trust online connections as much as offline ones. For example, it's harder to break promise to someone you know in person. It's easier to help someone you have shaken hands with. Meeting someone you previously only knew online takes that virtual relationship to the next level. This is another reason it's important to network.

You can network everywhere. Anywhere there are people, there is a chance for you to network. It's not a game of knowing as many people as possible. The quality of relationships is more important than quantity. Networking may not be easy for everyone, but once you get used to it, it's rewarding. Networking is easier than you think. Keep in mind that you can (but don't have to) go to specific networking events. A user group is a good place to start. Why not arrive a little in advance to chat with other attendees? You can join the other members for a drink after the presentations; if they don't propose this, you can start the new tradition.

You probably have plenty of occasions to network. You can begin a discussion with people you don't usually talk to at work. Try going outside your usual circle of friends and colleagues. When you go to a meeting, do you always hang out with same four people? That's your comfort zone. Next time, sit by someone you normally don't talk to and start a conversation. You never know what will happen.

Conferences are also places to meet new people. I attend conferences to speak, of course, and I also go for the people I can meet, the connections I can make, and the network I can build. The talks are a bonus; the people are the real treasure for me. There are so many ways to connect with people. You can introduce yourself to the speaker after a session. You can chat with someone waiting in the lunch line. You can make a ton of new acquaintances at the conference party if there is one.

Tip   Conferences are a networking opportunity—get the most out of your ticket price.

There are lots of networking events out there. Most of the time, it will make sense to be with people from your industry, but depending on your target audience, whom you hang out with may depend on whom you want to meet. I got in touch with some potential customers by going to a local event that is professional blogger monthly social gathering, where people go to have a drink and converse. It's just a networking event—no presentations—but because those people were not developers, they were potential customers. Of course, even developers can be potential customers—they may not have the same expertise as you. That's the formula I copied to start my own monthly networking event for developers in my city. I thought the opportunity to get developers together, no matter which technologies they used, was missing, so I created the event. In the first four months, the group reached nearly 400 members. I'm not saying this to brag about my group. My point is that people, even developers, want to network, so go ahead: you won't be the only one.

Imagine you are at a networking event organized by a local coffee shop. You meet Henry, an expert photographer. You talk about what you do in life, so he reciprocates. You discuss the fact that this coffee shop is your second office. Henry laughs. He often comes here to touch up pictures after a contract. You have a great discussion, and you like this guy. You ask him for his business card. You don't have any opportunities for him right now, but who knows what might happen in the future? In the end, you don't know if he is a good photographer, but he was a nice guy, and he seems to like his job, so why not get his contact in case you or your network need a professional photographer in the future?

Now imagine another scene: you are at the same networking event, just after you meet Henry. You meet Sophia, who is also a professional photographer. After introducing yourselves, Sophia starts to talk about her job. She gives you her business card and explains all the offers she has right now. She says it's a good time to book her, as she has some super special pricing going on—a deal you shouldn't miss! She shows you some pictures, even though you didn't say you were looking for a photographer. After 10 minutes, you tell her you want to continue to meet new people, thank her for her time, and say goodbye. Before you walk away, she remembers to ask you to contact her if you need a photographer.

At first sight, Sophia seems to be more professional than Henry. She was proactive. But was she too proactive? It's a matter of preference, but who will you remember in two months when a friend asks you if you know a good photographer? Will you remember Sophia, who pushed her offer down your throat? Or will you remember Henry, with whom you had an interesting discussion about photography, your work, and the coffee shop you nearly live in? I'll bet it will be Henry, because you didn't feel any pressure from him. Note that Sophia showed you some pictures she took, and they were good, but you don't even know if Henry is a good photographer! The thing is, you created a deeper connection with Henry. I wouldn't go as far as to say you became friends, but your interaction was more human, less business-minded, and friendlier. Of course, since it's your reputation you're putting on the table, you can't guarantee your friend that Henry is the best photographer you ever saw, but you can certainly put him in contact by saying you met this pleasant person.

Networking is important, but don't be a business card ninja: don't be that person who pushes the business card right away, like Sophia. There is nothing more annoying than saying hi to someone, and even before they finish replying, they are giving you their business card. Be more like Henry: enjoy the time with people and be passionate about what you do, but don't be annoying. Not everybody is worth adding to your network. It may sound harsh, but to target the right people and have a manageable network (remember, you need to maintain it), you have to choose your relations carefully. After all, you're not friends with everybody.

You can also network without networking. What do I mean? Simply that you can network and meet new people without a particular idea in mind. It's okay not to always talk business. It's okay not to always try to find new customers. Often, if you don't put that pressure on yourself and your conversation partner, you end up having a bigger impact.

Tip   As proud as you may be about the new design of your business card or a new offer you just published on your site, humanize your approach when you're in a networking situation.

Never Eat Alone

I recently finished reading the book *Never Eat Alone: And Other Secrets to Success, One Relationship at a Time* by Keith Ferrazzi and Tahl Raz (Crown Business, 2014). As the title suggests, it's a book about networking and how to be successful. What struck me the most was the first part of the title: never eat alone. It's simple and powerfully brilliant. It can be as simple as asking a friend to lunch. You could have lunch with someone you barely know, or a customer you haven't seen in a while. When I'm traveling, I notify people I'll be in their city during that period, and if they want to meet for lunch, dinner, beer, or coffee, I will be more than happy to do so if my schedule lets me. Maximize your time and always try to network.

Mentee and Mentor

If you have some experience in your industry, consider mentoring someone new or someone with less experience. It could involve improving in a particular programming language or landing the perfect job. Don't be shy. You have the experience and expertise. Why not help them benefit from it? Quite often, I answer questions or go out for a coffee with people who want some insights on the industry, tricks to land a new job, or ideas for their projects. I also mentor people on a regular basis: I meet with them once a month in person or on Skype. They often prepare questions or topics they want to discuss. Of course, I don't know everything, but sometimes mentoring is more about opening some doors, offering a different point of view, and sharing experience. People in my network know I'm happy to go out for a coffee or a drink to brainstorm or give some feedback on their ideas. As long as my schedule gives me the opportunity, it's a way for me to give back to the community. Mentoring takes time, so you need to have a good balance between giving back to people and doing everything else.

It works the other way, too. No matter where you are in your professional or personal life, and no matter where you are with your own brand, you should have a mentor—someone who will be able to guide you, who will be there for you when you need it, who has more or complementary experience, who has acquired some wisdom, and who can help you reach the next level. It can be a friend, a colleague, a speaker you met. It's not a sign of weakness to have a mentor. Quite the opposite. The relationship does not need to be permanent. You can work with a mentor for weeks, months, or years.

At some point, your mentor may not fit you and your goals anymore. I had a mentor when I was at Microsoft. We met every two to four weeks. The relationship was important to me, because he had been an employee there for many years and had held different positions in various departments. I needed this kind of mentorship, because I had to understand this special company. It helped me a lot, but when I left the company, as wise as he was, there was little point in continuing. We are still friends, but he is no longer my mentor.

Finding a good mentor is not easy. You need to find someone who understands you and with whom you are comfortable enough to talk about the good things and the bad ones. You will need to share your fears and ideas, too. A year later, I still don't have a new mentor. I have many people who help me day to day, but I don't have someone who officially took the role of my mentor. It is better to have no one than the wrong person. Still, I keep my eyes open to see who could be the next person to help me and guide me to the next level.

Never Burn a Bridge

No matter the situation, don't leave in bad terms. You never know when you will meet those people again or whether that previous employer of yours will end up a customer of yours in the future. You never know if that jerk of a coworker might be the superstar you want in your team in a couple of years (if she or he changes, of course).

When I decided to leave my last position, it was because I was not happy with my job at that point. I could have decided to stop doing the things I did not want to do anymore. After all, in a couple of weeks, I would be out, working at a new place. I decided to continue to do my job as well as I could until my last day. That meant I left on a high note, reaching the yearly goals I had to accomplish in that role and, more important, keeping in excellent contact with everyone in the company. I still have many people in my network from this period of my life; some of them I meet at different events. It would be awkward to be in the same room with people I shut the door on. You never know when you will work with those people again.

Before that, when I decided to find a new job after my first professional one as a developer, I did not burn any bridges. Guess what? Three years later, when I became a freelancer, I was in discussions with the same company I had worked with to freelance on some of their projects. If I had stayed a freelancer longer, we would have worked together, and I would have had another customer in my portfolio, not to mention another source of revenue.

Of course, there is always an exception that proves the rule. Some people may not be worth it. There are some people I consider toxic. Don't invest your time in toxic people or situations. It's not working. They don't like you. You don't like them. They are not nice people. Don't lose time with them. Sometimes it's not worth it to try and keep that door open when someone is trying to close it for you. Focus your energy where it matters.

Influence the Influencers

Are you the most brilliant person in the room? If the answer is yes, you are not in the right room. I always try, when possible, to be the dumbest person in the room. It's not that I consider myself stupid; I just want to improve myself. One way to get better at a sport, as everyone knows, is to play against someone better than you. You force yourself to give 100 percent just to stay even with them. What about when you are way better than your opponent? Boring. You don't have to give 100 percent. It's not even challenging.

It's the same thing for your brand, your expertise, and your professional life: if you want to get better, hang with people who are better than you, more brilliant, more successful, more connected. By doing so, you will challenge yourself, learn from others, and grow your network with people who can have an impact on your brand.

Who is the most brilliant person you know? It may be someone you don't know personally. Go talk to her or him. Send an email or an invite her for a coffee. Hang out at a conference. Be inspired. Ask this person to be your mentor.

Tip To get better, to reach the next level, hang out with the big dogs on the block.

There are also people called *influencers*. Their brand, mixed with their network, gives them access to many people, and because they are trusted, they can influence other people. What happened when the developer you liked so much at that conference was talking about that cool library you should use? You probably tried it when you got back home or to your office. You trusted him; he influenced you. Companies are always trying to work with influencers. Guess what? You are an influencer. We are all influencers. By growing your network and working on your brand, you will become a more important influencer with a bigger impact. I'm not talking about being a manipulator; by staying yourself and sharing your knowledge and opinions, you will influence others.

It's not just about hanging with the cool kids. It's not about being a groupie who puts high-visibility friends in their pocket or being in the right cliques. It's not about getting a network that has a bigger value in front of others or doing some name dropping. It's about growing a network that will help you grow.

Cherish Your Network

You now have a network. You've built a tribe. You know the persona you need to target. You're not done yet. You need to *cherish* your network, take care of it, and maintain it.

With some people, this happens automatically. You see them quite often. They are friends. You work with them. They're return customers. You cross their paths at conferences. It's easy—you stay in touch with them no matter what. But what about other contacts, the ones you haven't worked with in a while? The people from your previous job, whom you haven't talked to in years, or the customer who asked you for something you couldn't help them with at the time. You need to keep in touch with those people, too. What about the people you don't know yet? The ones who follow you on Twitter. The people who like your Instagram pictures and blog posts, even the bad ones. You need to cultivate them, too. It may be a lot of work to give them some love, but it's part of the job. Indulge me: a network is like a garden. If you don't tend it, don't nourish and maintain it, if you neglect it, it will die by itself, and no delicious vegetables or beautiful flowers for you.

Happily, there are tools to help you stay in touch with your network. Many customer relationship management (CRM) tools out there can help you. Right now, I'm using a tool called Nimble (http://nimble.com/) to help me keep in touch with my network. It helps me categorize my network with some keywords like *PHP*, *Bangalore*, and *startups*. I can also define by period how often I want to keep in touch with specific people: every week, every month, every year. It syncs with my social media, my agenda, and my email. In all these ways, it keeps me up to date with my connections and tracks when I last connected with them. I want to be sure I'll nourish my network and keep a healthy relation with the relevant people I care about.

It's Not Just About Who You Know

Like it or not, the software development world is kind of like high school. Groups form, and the golden boys and girls of the cool cliques have an easier life: better work, more prominence, and greater stature. Guess what? You can be part of that crowd and get the benefits that accrue: getting invited to the right conferences, being asked to write a book or give a speech, getting recommended for a consulting job, and so on. People who know you are as important as people you know.

A while ago I received an email inviting me to a conference in London. I did not know the conference, and I would never have thought to submit a talk there because it was a Java-centric event. (I used to do Java many years ago, but do not have a strong interest in it right now.) The conference had a big theme and welcomed anything else web-related, with talks on other technologies, like HTML. One of the organizers invited me, as she knew me from her previous company and I had written an article for them. I would have never received this offer if she didn't know me. I had a great experience speaking at this amazing conference and visiting London for the first time.

Maybe you want to participate in a project, but people didn't think of you first. Notify them of your interest. A studio was looking for a TV show host for show about the web, startups, and technology. I saw the announcement and contacted them. I had never hosted a television show before, though I have been on air as an expert to talk about some of my projects. Talking in front of people, being in front of a camera, and discussing the web, startups, and technology are part of what I do every day, even though I had no experience running a show in this medium. They probably had a lot of people contact them, because the concept was really interesting. One of the leads on the project knew me from a conference where I spoke and thinks the role would be perfect for me. The other partner did not know me, but it's easy to look at my blog and LinkedIn profile to see if I might be a good fit. We are still working on the details, but it could be another amazing project that fits with my brand and will help me gain visibility.

What Are You Waiting For?

I know. There's still one chapter left, but as soon as you can, go build your network. Create it online with tools like Twitter, Facebook, Google+, Pinterest, Instagram, Hacker News, LinkedIn, your blog, and any other sites or online communities that fit your brand. Build it offline, too. Don't put all your eggs in one basket. Offline community is critical to your success, so make new contacts, friends, and customers. Find the people you can help, and the people who can help you grow. Go to conferences, talk to people at user groups, and create networking events (but don't be that business card ninja).

The purpose of this group of people is to help you grow, but never forget that it's not just about you. If you always take and never give, this equation won't work. Finally, remember: it's better to be alone than in bad company.

CHAPTER 8

Work Your Magic
Lead with Your Personal Brand

With great power comes great responsibility.

—Spider-Man (borrowed from Voltaire)

I hope you are excited! You are building your story by working on your personal branding. You are taking your professional life to the next level, and that is not trivial.

Early in the book, you learn what personal branding is. Has your perception about it changed? You've also learned about the importance of thinking about your brand and being conscious of the fact that whether or not you care about it, you have a brand, so you had better be in control of it. Has the book helped alleviate any fears you had about looking egocentric, frivolous, or not humble in thinking about your brand, desiring recognition from you peers, and achieving visibility? We can agree that this is a first-world problem, but since we are lucky enough to care about it, let's take that chance and empower ourselves to live a better life, reach new goals, and have a better professional career.

I hope you've had a chance to learn more about yourself and the foundation of your brand. It's not always easy to take time and reflect on yourself. Often you are not yet where you would like to be or who you would like to become, but it's never too late. I hope that by reading this book, you've taken a step toward achieving your destiny. At the very least, you've defined what your dream personal brand would look like. Your brand may not be there yet, but you have already started to work on it.

Many tools are available to you, and you will do amazing work with them. Most important, I hope you have changed your mind about networking. You may have chosen a job in which most of your interaction is digital, but to get to the next level, you have to dust off your social skills and use them. Remember, the tribe is a critical asset for your success.

As developers, the world is ours. Let's take it!

Tip Don't wait until you have time to work on your brand or for the so-called right moment. The "right moment" is a fence that people set up so they have an excuse not to do something. Do it now.

Remove the Friction

Starting to work on your brand doesn't mean you need to do everything as soon as you can. When people want to get back in shape, they are often so motivated they take huge steps, like going to the gym five times a week after a period of doing nothing. This approach doesn't work because it's not sustainable. Instead, take small steps. Go to the gym once a week in the beginning, then two days a week, gradually adding more to your routine. That way, you increase your odds of success. It's the same concept for personal branding: start with baby steps so as not to burn yourself out. There are plenty of things you can do, plenty of tools you can use, but start slowly and choose wisely.

You need to make the process frictionless. (That's something you should keep in mind for everything in your life, in fact.) If there is too much friction in the process, you won't do it. Well, maybe you will do it, but not as often as you should, because you won't like it.

Remember If you don't have fun making your brand part of your life, you will fail.

What could cause friction? Maybe you followed my advice on using Twitter because I mentioned it's my blog's biggest source of views after search engines. Maybe you started using Twitter more, but you don't like it. Should you continue to use it in that case? No—even if it's working. Going out of your comfort zone doesn't mean doing things you really don't like—it's about silencing the little voice that says you are too afraid or not good enough to achieve something. If you don't like it, stop using it and move to the next thing: there are plenty of ways to get visibility online. This is what I'm doing with Google+. As a technical evangelist, I should be there because many developers use it. Some only use Google+—no Twitter, Facebook, or anything else. The problem is that I don't like it, so I'm not really using it. Use the tools that make sense to you.

Another source of friction can be how you use tools or applications—not the products or services themselves. For example, after a couple weeks of blogging, maybe you've found that you're not doing it as often as you were in the beginning. Maybe the excitement of blogging isn't there anymore, you don't have as many ideas about great topics, or you've just realized that blogging is not for you. It may just be that the blogging platform wasn't right for you. Try making a switch and removing the resistance between you and a published article. Changing the platform may be all you needed to do. If you still don't like it, that's okay. At least you know the platform wasn't the problem.

What's Next for You?

I sincerely hope what's next for you is nothing less than success. Recall back in Chapter 4, where you defined your goal, wrote it down with a timeline, and identified quantifiable ways of knowing whether you succeed. You will have to work on your brand, use the right tools, and make it happen. Nothing will happen by magic. You are the magic.

Remember Do you recall the impostor syndrome in Chapter 2—where you doubt that you're really worthy of success? You are not an impostor. You deserve success. You've worked for it. You've done amazing things with your ultimate goal in mind. Be happy and proud of what you achieved.

Lead with Your Brand

With great power comes great responsibility, said a well-known man. You have (or soon will have) power. You will not rule the world, but if you do, remember you read my book and I'm an ally, a friend! You will gain power in different ways, and you need to be responsible about using it.

First, you will become a bigger influence. The more your network grows, the more people you influence. Of course, you can't be called an influencer just by the number of people in your network. People need to trust you and believe in what you say, your opinion, your skills, and your expertise. You will become a leader. By doing so, you have the responsibility of becoming a role model. People will look to you for guidance and inspiration. They may want to do what you've done and be like you. You need to keep your integrity. For example, if your blog becomes very successful, a company may contact you about blogging about their products or invite you to special events. You need to think carefully about that. Don't get me wrong—I like to get free stuff, be invited to VIP events, and be the first to know or try something. Those are all cool benefits of being classified as an influencer. But you need to stay honest with your audience. If you don't like a product or service, say so. Don't say it was all beautiful with unicorns all over the place if that is not true. Fluffing up the truth or outright lying to people may work for a while, but you will eventually lose your credibility. Without credibility, you will slowly lose your network. Your brand will suffer and could even become something negative. You may want accept those offers—I often do—and it's nice, but be honest and transparent with your audience about it.

Second, you need to stay true to yourself no matter what. If you start to lie to yourself, it will be the beginning of the end. That means you may want to refuse some projects if they don't make sense for you, even if it's something that will help you make a huge leap in your career or will crucially elevate your brand. When you say yes, be sure you're saying yes for the right reasons. The TV show I might host is a tremendous opportunity. It will give me great visibility in a medium where I have had none. I want to host the show, not because it's on TV but because it's about the web, startups, and technology—things that are an important part of my life. I would not have proposed myself for the job just for the sake of being on television (even if that's a nice thing).

Being approached can happen in different ways. When Microsoft approached me four years ago about an open position in Canada, I turned them down three times before meeting one person on the team to talk to about the job. I had to be honest with myself. At that time, my vision of the company was not entirely positive. Having started as a freelancer about six months prior, I was not looking for a job. At the same time, the company wanted to talk to me about becoming what I still see today as my dream job: technical evangelist. The evangelist I met in the Montreal office did an amazing job of explaining the role to me and the company's vision for someone like me. If it weren't for that conversation, I would never have worked for Microsoft, and I may not have gotten to be where I am today. In the end, I accepted the job not for the paycheck or because it was an excellent springboard for me. I accepted because on balance, doing so respected my values, and I was able to stay true to myself. I promoted the open source mind-set inside Microsoft while educating Canadian developers about the openness of the company. I stayed until I was no longer able to stay true to myself.

Don't Get Too Comfortable

I've talked about doing things outside your comfort zone. I would add that you should not become too comfortable even with your own brand. That may sound stupid—you've worked hard to reach the point where you are right now. By setting the personal goal of not getting too comfortable with your brand, you give yourself the permission to always go forward and to always look for more.

Success in Programming

> **Remember** Things change. So should you. There is always something you can do better, always something you can improve on, and always a next level to reach.

In college, my classes had three types of people. People like me, who never really had professional jobs and were studying to enter the market. A second group were a bit older and came from different industries; they wanted the option to change: being a programmer seemed like a good choice for them. A third category of students was made up of developers with many years of experience. Why did those developers came to school even though they probably had more experience under the belt than the teacher? Many of them had an expertise in only one programming language or one type of system and were not finding jobs related to that expertise.

One example that comes to mind is those who were doing AS400 at a time when AS400 expertise was not needed much. Too many developers had that expertise, and not enough jobs were available. They had to come back to school to update their skills and prove to future employers they were able to code with new technology. These were some of the darkest years for the industry—many developers lost their jobs after the dot-com bubble burst. My point is that you should always try to learn new things and keep up to date with the industry. If they had done that during their careers, maybe they wouldn't have had to come back to school.

From my first day at my first job until today, I have used a lot of technologies: Java, Perl, PHP, C# for web such as Windows Mobile, Java for Blackberry, Objective-C for iOS, HTML, CSS, JavaScript, and more. Right now, I'm all about HTML and the web. As much as I care and believe in the web and its technologies, no one knows where they will be in a few years. Never be afraid of learning new things: be curious about new technology, new frameworks, and what's coming next. The next technology could be the one that will help you build your amazing application idea, land a new job, or keep your present one. Adapt or die, as some might say.

You can also take risks. Taking risks can be rewarding, but isn't always. Think about the people who were the first to get behind Apple's iPhones and use the first SDK to create applications. They got an experience faster than anyone else and, probably because not too many were developing for iOS at the beginning, gained credibility and visibility. Of course, today being an iOS developer is not uncommon—just look at the number of apps in the App Store: more than a million. On the other hand, living on the edge can be tricky. I have some friends who built their business on just one technology. It worked well until it didn't work well. When the company behind that technology decided to kill the product, it was not easy for the business. Happily they were able to move forward (and are now even more successful), but keep in mind that the opposite can happen just as easily.

Knowing When to Move On

Knowing when to quit is an underrated skill. Just because you volunteer doesn't mean you should give them your time forevermore. What happens if it's not working for you? You don't work somewhere for 20 years just because you adhere to the organization's mission. Sometimes it's better to leave than to do bad work. Doing bad work means not giving your 100 percent, not, as Seth Godin would say, creating art. It's also good to know yourself and what your limits are.

When I was freelancer, I focused on web development and mobile development. I wanted my brand to focus on that last expertise: mobility. So I decided to volunteer at a conference and be responsible for creating a new track about mobility, filled with sessions on mobile development in all its forms. It was a great project, and the conference organizers were happy about my offer. Before starting work on that project, I realized that building this enterprise was going to be a lot of work, especially at the beginning stage, where I was. I thought I would be able to do both well, but realized I wouldn't be able to deliver quality results like I always do. So I decided to quit before it was too late. The organizers were not happy, but because I let them know so quickly, it gave them time to find someone else. They would have been quite angry had I stayed and produced crappy results. Sometimes, continuing something doesn't make sense anymore. Know when to leave, and know when to stop.

I've noticed that friends who have volunteered in organizations often won't quit, even when they would like to. It's as if they are afraid the organization will close after they leave, or they feel guilty about no longer volunteering. Remember: no one is irreplaceable. It may be hard to accept, but any organization will likely survive your departure.

Know yourself. I know I am a starter, a serial entrepreneur. I get very excited when I have a new idea, a new project to start. I put a lot of energy in the project to make it happen. After it's working well and has real success, I get bored. It's annoying, but it's a reality that I'm like that, and I know myself well enough to understand that. It's why I've started festivals, user groups, podcasts, and other events—but afterward, I have left or handed the project over to someone else. When you know yourself, it's easier to manage these situations and know when to quit.

When you know yourself well, it's also easier to set expectations. I was talking with Noah Redler, the Notman House (http://notman.org) director, about a project we will do together. (If you ever come to Montreal, stop and say hello; many developers and startups work and hang out at the Notman House, and many events happen between their walls.) I set the expectation right at the beginning: it's a nice project, I want to do it, you will help me, it will work, but once it reaches its full potential, I will find someone to replace me because

I'll get bored. It sounds weird to have a discussion like that, but as far as I know, Noah saluted my honesty and was entirely happy with this proposition. As long as you don't leave people in trouble, it's feasible.

Who Is Talking About You?

It's a fact: you will gain more visibility and your tribe will help you do so. You may write great blog posts that will interest other people or media. An attendee at a conference you spoke to may write a blog post and highlight your presentation. You might create an open-source library that will change how developers work, and Hacker News will make you a celebrity for a day. There are many ways that you can get visibility.

Setting Alerts

It's good to have someone praise what you did (or complain about something you said) in front of you, but in my experience, not many people will criticize someone face to face. Would you like to know when someone writes about you or some of your project on the web? There are tools that can notify you when someone uses specific keywords or points to one of your properties. I watch for when people talk about me or one of my projects or points my site. For most of them, I use a tool call Google Alerts (www.google.com/alerts). You can also use tools like Talkwalker Alerts (www.talkwalker.com/alerts).

I set an alert on my name, even using different spellings: my real name, Frédéric Harper, how non–French speakers write it (Frederic Harper), and also as Fred Harper, because people usually call me Fred. As any SEO expert can tell you, it's less about how you think people search for your expertise or service type than it is about how people really search.

I also set alerts for various projects I have. Many people won't notify you if they write an article about you or about something you did. If you have a common name or your project or group uses familiar words, you may get many alerts that are irrelevant. It's better to have false alerts than miss the real ones. Recently I was able to correct some inaccurate facts about an event I created because I received an alert about it.

It's good to know what people are saying about you. It gives you the opportunity to react to anything quickly if you need to or even just thank people. Remember, they don't owe you anything, so take the time to thank people who share your posts, write about your project, and support you.

Scanning Twitter

Because I use Twitter a lot, it's one of the places I regularly look for communications about me or any of my projects. Tweets don't seem to be indexed by search engines, so you need to use Twitter's search tool. I use Tweetdeck (https://about.twitter.com/products/tweetdeck) as my client for Twitter. I can add a column with search terms. As soon as a tweet contains one of those terms, it shows in that column so I can reply or just thank the person. It's interesting to start conversations like this. I used some of the same terms as in Talkwalker. Even if my Twitter ID is listed everywhere (on my first as well as my last slides of all my presentations, on my business card, on my site) and even though you can search for my name on Twitter and will quickly find it, many people don't link to that account in their Tweets, and that will be the same for you. It happens quite often in conferences, so by looking for my name, and not just my Twitter ID, I can find content I would not have been aware of. Of course, with all those alerts I set, some of them won't be about me, some may be spam, and some of them, like people using @fharper on Twitter when pointing to my blog, could have been found elsewhere, but I'm catching many I would not have known about otherwise. Stay alert as to what people share about you and your projects.

Quantify Your Impact with Metrics

No matter what your end goal is, I've challenged you to add a timeline to it, break it into smaller steps, and make it quantifiable. You need and want to know when you will succeed because that will help you make it happen. There are many ways to measure how you will be successful, and only you can define them. This section mentions three tools you can use. These tools are probably the three most popular right now.

Numbers: More Important than You Think

I don't care much about numbers, but it seems the rest of the world does. (For me, it's always been more about quality than quantity.) That said, someone with 40,000 followers probably has more visibility and a bigger brand presence than someone with 10,000. Numbers can be a good way to see if you are building a tribe and getting great visibility.

You can easily see how many Facebook friends you have. You can also check the number of people who have added you to their Google+ circles. The same thing goes for your followers on Twitter, and you can measure the number of people who favorite your tweets, the number of mentions you get, and even the number of retweets. One of the tools I use for Twitter is Favstar.

fm (http://favstar.fm), shown in Figure 8-1. As you can see, Favstar gives me some statistics about my Twitter account and I can easily find my most popular tweets.

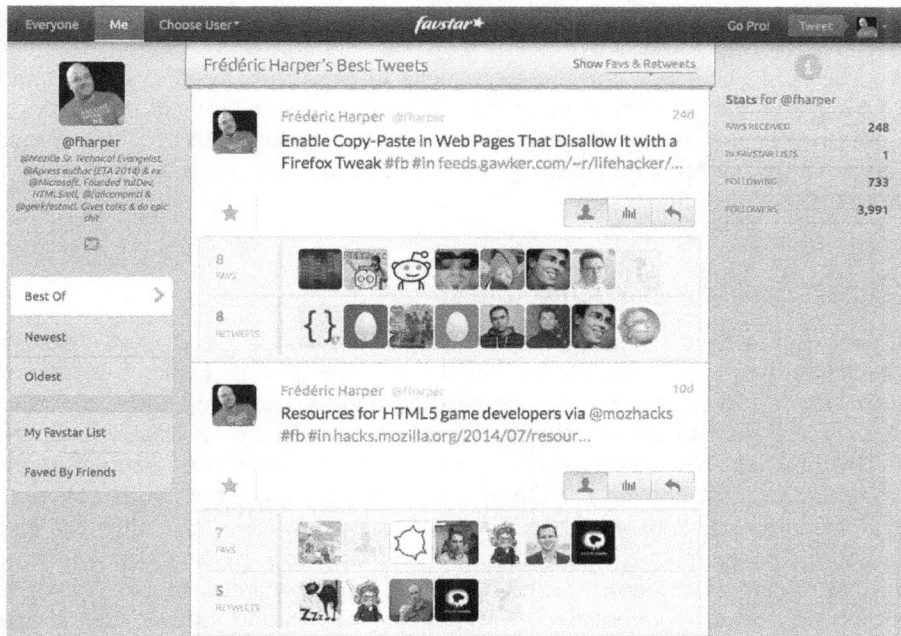

Figure 8-1. My Favstar account

You can add some analytics tools to your blog, such as Google Analytics (www.google.com/analytics/). Even if you don't care so much about the numbers, it's always interesting to know where people come from and what key words bring them to your site. I'm always curious to see which of my posts were the most popular, and that's a statistic you get with analytics tools. It can help you see what your audience likes. Maybe there is a special type of post that works better than the others. Sometimes it's a bit sad to see that the number of views are low for an article you were particularly proud of.

Klout Me, I'm Famous

Klout (https://klout.com) gives you a score that seems to be mostly based on the numbers of followers and the "noise" you make, such as how often you share things on your accounts connected to the service. I'm not sure you can define someone's influence with an algorithm. That's not frustration about the fact that my Klout score is not that high—in fact it's not bad at all, I had 69 last time I checked. For the data geeks in the room, people with a score of 63 are in the top 5% of all users. Many people use Klout as a reference. Some companies even give perks to people with higher Klout scores. I've seen job postings ask for a minimum Klout score to apply. Klout is another way of measuring your influence.

Open Source Report Card

Open Source Report Card (http://osrc.dfm.io/) is a tool that creates a report on your participation and activity on GitHub (see Figure 8-2). It puts into words something that can be hard to understand: your GitHub profile. A technical person won't have any problem understanding what you do on GitHub by looking at your profile, but what about the HR department of the company you just applied to? Open Source Report Card puts your contribution in perspective. In my full report, you can learn that I'm mainly creating JavaScript projects, but I did some PHP and C#. You can see that I created my own projects and contributed mainly to other projects. Report Card also shows you other developers on GitHub that you should follow. You can use this tool to give others an idea of what you do on GitHub.

THE OPEN SOURCE REPORT CARD

 fharper

fharper is an exceptional JavaScripter who loves pushing code. fharper is a nine-to-fiver who works best in the morning (around 11 am).

fharper's developer personality is very similar to oroce's but oroce spends more of their time commenting on issues. There is also an uncanny similarity between fharper's activity stream and those of jakiestfu, dybskiy, David Chase, and dendril.

It seems like fharper is—or should be—friends with marti1125. With this in mind, it's worth noting that marti1125 is a more serious forker. There is also an obvious connection between fharper and rnowm, luke crouch, rwaldron, and gasolin.

These days, fharper is most actively contributing to the repositories: kaaes/work_from_cafe, fharper/FirefoxOS-Paint, fharper/HTML5challenges001-canvas_fileapi, robnyman/Firefox-OS-Boilerplate-App, and fharper/Firefox-OS-Boilerplate-App.

STATISTICS

The two following graphs show fharper's average weekly and daily schedules. These charts give significant insight into fharper's character as a developer. The colors in the charts indicate the fraction of events that are **watching**, **pushes**, **issue comments**, **new repos or branches**, and **pull requests**.

Figure 8-2. Section of my Open Source Report Card

More Than One Brand?

Can you have more than one brand? Yes and no. The truth is, you have only one brand. From time to time that brand will change as you gain experience and when you set new goals. On the other hand, you can have a variant of your brand—or different sections or parts of your brand—depending on what you want to achieve and where you are. No matter how many variations you have, they will all be related.

Remember my elevator pitch?

> Sr. Technical Evangelist at Mozilla, web lover, T-shirt geek, music aficionado, public speaker, social beast, blogger, and doing epic shit!

My elevator pitch is part of my brand. It's how I define myself, and it may not be my end goal. Being a technical evangelist is my job, but I don't want my brand to be tied to just my job. Who knows what I will do next year, or 3 years or 10 years from now? It's like creating a persona to get a job. It might not be the persona you want to reach for all parts of your brand. This shouldn't be too confusing. From what you know about me, you can tell that the ultimate umbrella of my brand is that I'm a doer, and I like to do epic shit. Being an evangelist is part of this overall concept, but I was doing all kinds of stuff when I was a developer, too. I can do great things; I can achieve good stuff with other kinds of people. So can you.

What to Read Next?

Lots of books can help you with your brand—even certain novels. For nonfiction, I already mentioned some specific books I liked that I think could help you. Here they are again:

- *Never Eat Alone, Expanded and Updated: And Other Secrets to Success, One Relationship at a Time* by Keith Ferrazzi and Tahl Raz (Crown Business, 2014).
- *The Flinch* (Domino Project, 2011) by Julien Smith.
- *Tribes: We Need You to Lead Us* by Seth Godin (Portfolio Hardcover, 2008).
- *Impact Equation: Are You Making Things Happen or Just Making Noise?* (Portfolio, 2012) by Julien Smith and Chris Brogan.

Here are some more books that could help you go further with some topics on this book:

- *Ctrl Alt Delete: Reboot Your Business. Reboot Your Life. Your Future Depends On It* by Mitch Joel (Business Plus, 2013). This book is about adapting to the new world. I think this book is more for marketing people, but it's interesting to read, and we can learn much from this brilliant guy.
- *Do the Work* by Steven Pressfield (Domino Project, 2011) is all about, as the title says, doing the work. It goes in the same direction as *The Flinch* by Julien Smith.
- *Free: The Future of a Radical Price* by Chris Anderson (Hyperion, 2009) is an excellent book if you want to understand the free culture and the marketing impact it can have on your business and work. It's interesting from an open-source and free software perspective, too.
- *The Icarus Deception: How High Will You Fly?* by Seth Godin (Portfolio Hardcover, 2012). This is an interesting book to think about how you can achieve your end goal, which is often the topic of Seth's books.
- *Purple Cow, New Edition: Transform Your Business by Being Remarkable* by Seth Godin (Portfolio Hardcover, 2009). The focus of this book is business, but remember, you can adapt all those books to yourself and to your brand. You can be remarkable. In the end, isn't that the goal of working on your personal brand?
- *Remote: Office Not Required* by Jason Fried and David Heinemeier Hansson (Crown Business, 2013). This is a good book to read if you ever think of working at home, having a discussion with your boss about it, or starting a remote working culture in your business.
- *Rework* (Crown Business, 2010), again by Jason Fried and David Heinemeier Hansson, is one of the most interesting books I've read in a while. It will help you think how you can perform better, faster, and more easily accomplish your tasks (or your business if you have one) by not staying in the old way of doing things. It's a good book, even if you don't own a business. If you only read one book in this list, make it this one.
- *Six Pixels of Separation: Everyone Is Connected. Connect Your Business to Everyone* by Mitch Joel (Business Plus, 2009). I think the title says it all.

- *The Wisdom of Crowds: Why the Many Are Smarter Than the Few and How Collective Wisdom Shapes Business, Economies, Societies and Nations* by James Surowiecki (Doubleday, 2004). Since your tribe will be an important part of your brand, it's interesting to understand how the crowd is working and how most of the time the wisdom comes from the crowd.
- *Crush It!: Why NOW Is the Time to Cash In on Your Passion* by Gary Vaynerchuk (HarperStudio, 2009) is all about making your passion your breadwinner. After all, isn't that what managing his personal brand is all about? Gary has some other books you may want to check out as well.
- *Switch: How to Change Things When Change Is Hard* by Chip Heath and Dan Heath (Random House Canada, 2010) is a book about change: how to work with your rational and emotional minds to make change in your life.

You'll notice that these books are not about what we do every day—developing software—though technical books can help your brand, too. Your expertise is probably creating applications. Also note that the books I've listed are not necessarily labeled as being about personal branding. They help you market yourself (or often your company, but many things can apply to yourself), be better or more efficient, network, get out of your comfort zone, work remotely, and more. Because of that, they all are very helpful when it comes to working on your brand.

The Beginning of a Journey

I can't repeat myself enough: personal branding is the beginning of an amazing journey, of something big. This book is not the end but the start of something wonderful. You will set goals and work toward reaching them. You will become someone new by staying yourself. When you think you are done, that your brand is strong enough, continue to make it stronger. When you think you have reached your goal and are satisfied with what you have, continue with a new, higher goal. When you are tired, and the results are not coming as fast as you would like, keep going. When you think your elevator pitch is perfect, keep working on it. When you think you have the right audience and a good number of people in your tribe, continue to network. When you think you know everything you have to know, continue to educate yourself and improve your day-to-day life.

A book is a frozen moment in time. Some of the tools I've recommended here may not be in use forever. Maybe some of the services I've recommended will vanish and be replaced by others. That can't be helped. Keep in mind that the concepts I've shared here will always be true. Personal branding will remain the key to your success.

When I decided to write this book, I believed that others could to benefit from my experience. I'm happy with my life and career and I would like everybody to be as happy as I am. Maybe I'm a dreamer, but I want all developers to reach their full potential. One way to do this is to use personal branding: the brand you already have, the brand that you will work on to reach the next level, to unleash the power inside you. There is enough room on the stage for all of us.

I wish you all the best, and remember… do epic shit!

Yours truly,

Frédéric Harper

Index

A

Achieving, personal brand
    action, importance of, 57
    area of expertise, 65
    A/S/L, 68
    being passionate, 53
    blogs, use of, 60
    comfort zone, 62
    custom icon, 61
    denying request from others, 58–60
    examples, 56–57
    fear of missing out (FOMO), 64
    giving time, 67
    giving work instead of time, 67–68
    management, brand, 53
    not being afraid of asking, 63–64
    opinions, 62
    piece of art, 61
    planning, 53
    saying 'no' to others, 59
    scrum framework, 60
    starting to work, 60
    taking easiest path, 63
    user groups, connecting with, 61
Alerts, setting, 143
A/S/L (age, sex, location), 68–69

B

"Being yourself" philosophy, 22
Blog, creating, 120
Blogging, 83
    blogosphere, 88
    collateral benefits, 84
    commenting, 88
    editorial line, 86
    expectations, 86
    guest blogging, 88
    platform, 85–86
    sharing passion, 88
    showing expertise, 84
    to get started, 85
    Wordpress, 85
Blogging Wordpress documentation, 86
Blogosphere, 88
Books
    for further reading, 148–150
    writing, 103
Brand
    actual brand, 43–44
    defining, 33
    developers, branding for, 34
    differentiating, importance, 42–43
    example, 48–49
    exercise for proper brand, 46–47
    GitHub, 47
    improvement, 47
    past experience, 44
    people with strong brands, comparing, 43
    professional side, 44–45
    reaching goal through branding, 34–35
    redefining elevator pitch, 49–50
    self, differentiating, 42
    updating own brand, 45
Bugzilla, 90, 113

Index

C

Camtasia, 102
Comfort zone, 62, 140
Conferences, 106, 129
Consistent, being, 107–108
Content
    creation, 73–74
    sources, 73
Customer relationship management (CRM) tools, 135

D

Dribbble, 95, 113
    design skills, 95
    Lea Verou's Dribbble profile, 96

E

Elevator pitch, 23
    definition, 23
    example, 23–27
    exercise, 27–28
    refining, 27
An Event Apart (conference series), 79
Expertise, area of, 65

F

Facebook, 121
Failure at work, 68
Firefox OS documentation, 94
FOMO (fear of missing out), 64
Friction, 138
    cause, 138
    tools or applications, use of, 139

G

Ghost, 85
GitHub, 52, 89, 113
    bug tracker system, 90
    fixing bugs and pull requests, 90
    My Bugzilla profile, 91
    Profile's front page, 90

Goal
    breaking in action steps, 38
    change in goals, 41
    change in timeline, 41
    combination, easy and complex, 37
    defining, 35
    dream job, getting, 35
    interim goals, example, 40
    large and big, 38
    longer goals, 40
    management, as a goal, 37
    new goal timeline, 41
    paycheck, bigger, 36
    quantifiable, 38–39
    skills or competencies, building, 36
    splitting in steps, 38
    timeline
        example, 39–40
        timeline, setting, 39
    visibility, getting, 36
Google+, 121
Google, most used search engine, 71–73
Guest blogging, 88

H

Hacker News, 122
Happy Cog, 79
HTML in Toronto on Meetup.com, 98

I

Ideas, becoming projects, 65
Impact, actions, 54
The Impact Equation: Are You Making Things Happen or Just Making Noise?, 55
Instagram, 83
Internet Relay Chat (IRC), 68

J

jQuery Project, 116

K

Keystrokes, limited number, 74
Klout score, 146

L

Lanyrd, 113
Leadership, 116
Leading, with personal brand, 137–139
    analytics tools, 145
    being approached, 140
    being not too comfortable, 140–141
    being true, 140
    books to read, 148–150
    influence, 139
    Klout score, 146
    knowing self, 142–143
    knowing when to quit, 142
    metrics, 144
    more brands, 148
    number of connections, 144
    Open Source Report Card, 146–147
    scanning Twitter, 144
    setting alerts, 143
    visibility, gaining, 143
LinkedIn
    advantages, 128
    potential for professional connections, 128
    profile, 126, 128

M

Meetup, 113
Mentee and mentor, 132
Metrics, impact, 144
Mozilla Developer Network (MDN) profile, 95, 113

N

NameChk, username availability, 70
Network
    advice, 116
    being the best, 133–134
    cherishing, 134–135
    company culture, 117
    conferences, 129
    criteria, persona, 119
    events, 130–131
    influencers, 134
    leadership, 116
    maintaining good terms, 133
    mentee and mentor, 132
    networking events, creating, 136
    notifying interests, 135
    occasions to network, 129
    online relationships, 120
    personal branding, importance of, 115
    personal relationships, 129
    skills, experience, and talent, 118
    StackOverflow (tool), 120
    target audience, 118
    tribe, choosing, 118
    tribe member persona, 119
    without networking, 131
Never Eat Alone: And Other Secrets to Success, 131
Newsify, 109

O

One Relationship at a Time, 131
Online relationships, 120
Open source, 88
Open Source Report Card, 146–147
Optimizing, everything
    being informed, 108–112
        blogs and websites, Really Simple Syndication (RSS), 109
        ReadKit, 110
    focus, 112
        task management systems, 113
        working at home, 113
    tool box, 113
    trust on memory, 112
Outernet, 75

P, Q

Personal branding
    being, authentic, 21–22
    being unique, 31
    career, 7, 19

Personal branding (cont.)
  changes within, bringing, 23
  CSS and HTML5, 4–5
  description, 1, 9
  elevator pitch, 23
  feedback, 30
  Firefox browser, 2–3
  for developers, 51
  fun, 7–8
  goal, achieving, 20
  impostor syndrome, 14
  indispensability, 10–11
  job security and money, 6, 11
  languages, 6
  LinkedIn profile, 17
  magic, 17
  marketing agency, 4
  Maslow's hierarchy of needs, 13–14
  opinion, 14
  opportunities, 12
  people's perception, 29–30
  programming language, 14
  restaurants, 3
  self-improvement, 30–31
  strengths, focus on, 30
  technical evangelist, 15–16
  time, 7
Personality questions, 20
Podcasting, 104
  audio, 104
  video, 104–105
Professional recognitions
  certifications, 106
  Most Valuable Professional (MVP), Microsoft recognition, 107
Public speaking, 96, 99
  at conferences, 97
  benefits, 97
  camp event, 97
  clubs, 99
  speaker idol events, 99

R

ReadKit, 110
Really Simple Syndication (RSS), 109
Recording, 102–103

S

Scale
  combination with impact, 55
  network, use of, 56
  power of modern media, 56
Self-improvement, guidelines, 30–31
Shyness
  getting out of comfort zone, 75
  guidelines for losing, 76–77
Slashdot, 122
Slides
  sharing, 99, 101, 103
  SlideShare profile, 100, 113
Social media, 22–23
  channels, 67
  policies, 83
  sites
    Facebook, 122
    GitHub, 124
    Google+, 122
    Hacker News, design of, 123
    Instagram, 122
    LinkedIn, 126–128
    Snipplr, 124
    technical people, 122–125
    Twitter, 121
StackOverflow, 91, 93, 113
  firefox-os tag, 92
  to show expertise, 93
Strength Finder 2.0, 31
Strengths, focus on, 30–31

T

Technical wikis, 94
Tribes: We Need You to Lead Us, 117
Twitter, 121, 144
Typepad, 85

U

Unconference, organizing, 105
User groups, 106

V

Volunteering, 66

W, X, Y

Walsh, David (developer), advice, 51–52

Web technologies, 74

Wordpress, 85

Z

Zeldman, Jeffrey
    on career goals, 81–82
    on personal branding, 79

Get the eBook for only $10!

Now you can take the weightless companion with you anywhere, anytime. Your purchase of this book entitles you to 3 electronic versions for only $10.

This Apress title will prove so indispensible that you'll want to carry it with you everywhere, which is why we are offering the eBook in 3 formats for only $10 if you have already purchased the print book.

Convenient and fully searchable, the PDF version enables you to easily find and copy code—or perform examples by quickly toggling between instructions and applications. The MOBI format is ideal for your Kindle, while the ePUB can be utilized on a variety of mobile devices.

Go to www.apress.com/promo/tendollars to purchase your companion eBook.

All Apress eBooks are subject to copyright. All rights are reserved by the Publisher, whether the whole or part of the material is concerned, specifically the rights of translation, reprinting, reuse of illustrations, recitation, broadcasting, reproduction on microfilms or in any other physical way, and transmission or information storage and retrieval, electronic adaptation, computer software, or by similar or dissimilar methodology now known or hereafter developed. Exempted from this legal reservation are brief excerpts in connection with reviews or scholarly analysis or material supplied specifically for the purpose of being entered and executed on a computer system, for exclusive use by the purchaser of the work. Duplication of this publication or parts thereof is permitted only under the provisions of the Copyright Law of the Publisher's location, in its current version, and permission for use must always be obtained from Springer. Permissions for use may be obtained through RightsLink at the Copyright Clearance Center. Violations are liable to prosecution under the respective Copyright Law.

Other Apress Business Titles You Will Find Useful

The Coder's Path to Wealth and Independence
Beckner
978-1-4842-0422-1

Tech Job Hunt Handbook
Grossman
978-1-4302-4548-3

The Career Programmer
Duncan
978-1-5905-9624-1

Have Fun, Get Paid
Duncan
978-1-4302-6100-1

Design Thinking for Entrepreneurs and Small Businesses
Ingle
978-1-4302-6181-0

Financial Modeling for Business Owners and Entrepreneurs
Sawyer
978-1-4842-0371-2

Common Sense
Tanner
978-1-4302-4152-2

Disruption by Design
Paetz
978-1-4302-4632-9

Startup
Ready
978-1-4302-4218-5

Available at www.apress.com

GPSR Compliance
The European Union's (EU) General Product Safety Regulation (GPSR) is a set of rules that requires consumer products to be safe and our obligations to ensure this.

If you have any concerns about our products, you can contact us on

ProductSafety@springernature.com

In case Publisher is established outside the EU, the EU authorized representative is:

Springer Nature Customer Service Center GmbH
Europaplatz 3
69115 Heidelberg, Germany

www.ingramcontent.com/pod-product-compliance
Lightning Source LLC
LaVergne TN
LVHW012009260326
834688LV00057B/365